THE DESCENT INTO HELL

THE SEABURY LIBRARY OF CONTEMPORARY THEOLOGY

THE DESCENT INTO HELL

A Study of the Radical Reversal of the Christian Consciousness

THOMAS J. J. ALTIZER

A Crossroad Book
The Seabury Press · New York

1979
The Seabury Press
815 Second Avenue
New York, N.Y. 10017

Published 1970 by J.B. Lippincott Company
Seabury paperback edition 1979

Library of Congress Catalog Card Number: 79-88310
ISBN: 0-8164-1194-8

Printed in the United States of America

1. Christianity --20ᵗʰ Century

FOR ALMA

✳

Preface

*

A word is in order about the nature of the theological enterprise embodied in this book. On the one hand, it is an attempt to think radically about the contemporary meaning of the Christian faith. On the other hand, it is written with the conviction that Christianity has undergone a revolutionary transformation in the modern world, and the primary responsibility of the theologian is to come to understand the meaning of a new form of faith which is already manifest and real. Theological thinking cannot create a new form of faith: it can only record its advent, and undertake to derive from it a coherent and consistent symbolic and conceptual meaning. Christianity alone among the religions of the world has come to understand itself as a forward-moving and evolving form of faith. But our situation is such that it is no longer possible to understand an evolving form of faith as preserving its previous forms and expressions in their original and given identities. If we will not confess that

7

we have lost what we once knew as faith, then we will
not be open to a new and revolutionary world of faith.
Therefore a full acceptance of the dissolution of previous
forms of faith is an indispensable presupposition for initi-
ation into a new reality of faith.

It is in this historical context that a new meaning of
radical Christianity and radical faith has arisen before us.
No longer can we think of radical Christianity as a sectarian and reactionary movement to a presumed original or
primitive form of faith. On the contrary, it is a revolutionary movement to a new future, and to a future which has
already dawned in our present. While it is true that radical thinkers and visionaries have returned to the original
ground of the Christian faith—as witness Blake, Hegel,
Kierkegaard, and Dostoyevsky—they have done so as a
means of realizing that ground in a new and revolutionary form. So much is this the case that, with the possible
exception of Kierkegaard, theology has yet to establish
the Christian identity of such revolutionary thinking and
vision. This need not surprise us, for true revolutions are
only gradually accepted and understood by the worlds
which they confront. Despite the genuine achievements
of modern theology, we are still only at the threshold of
understanding a new and revolutionary world of faith.
We will fully enter that threshold only when we acknowledge that a revolutionary transformation of faith has already occurred. Then the contemporary Christian will be
prepared to accept not only the advent of a new world
but also the advent of a new form and identity of Christ.

After the passage of almost a century, we are now in a position to identify some if not all of the revolutionary thinkers and visionaries of the nineteenth century. At the very least, these include Blake, Hegel, Kierkegaard, Marx, Dostoyevsky, Nietzsche, and Freud. Although it is not yet possible to understand these revolutionary prophets as unveiling an identical or common world, it is possible to see that all shared a common method or form of thinking and vision. Hegel gave us not only a word but also a comprehensive logic for this method of thinking, and the word is "dialectic." Significantly enough, theology is the only intellectual discipline in the non-Communist world which has cultivated and practiced dialectical thinking. In large measure this is due to the fact that so many of the higher expressions of religion have assumed a dialectical form, and this is true not only of a Paul, an Augustine, and a Luther, but also of all of the purer or most total expressions of mystical and prophetic religion. These expressions of religion can offer a pure or total faith and vision only by way of an absolute reversal or dissolution of all existing or given forms of consciousness and experience. It is such a reversal or dissolution which lies at the center of dialectical thinking and vision. All too naturally modern revolutionary thinkers and seers have discovered and embodied various modes of such a dialectical reversal or dissolution, for only a radical negation and transcendence of the world of the past can make possible the advent and realization of a new world of the future.

Dialectical thinking and vision not only attempt to negate and transcend an established or given world of consciousness and society; they also attempt to annul or dissolve all those polarities and antinomies which alienate and isolate all individual centers of experience. Whether we turn to ancient or modern expressions of a dialectical way, we discover that it seeks out the lost or hidden ground of suffering and illusion. Spurning every partial or temporary assuagement of illusion and pain, it is in quest of the goal of total redemption or freedom. Accordingly, a dialectical way seeks to dissolve or reverse all those laws and categories which sanction and uphold an established mode of life. Wherever they have appeared, dialectical thinking and vision have been revolutionary, for they have assaulted the most deeply embedded principles and values of their world. There is no path for us into the meaning of a contemporary dialectical vision unless we are prepared to question our most deeply cherished convictions. Furthermore, we must also be prepared not only to question but also to abandon our established modes of thinking and analysis. There can be no doubt that this is a difficult if not impossible task for the nonrevolutionary thinker. Yet, at bottom, the task has already been accomplished—and accomplished, in its foundations, in the nineteenth century. Our task is only to appropriate this revolutionary accomplishment, and to appropriate it in such a way as to make it meaningful and real in our world.

This is no small task, however, and it is one which has

seldom been openly and directly confronted by theological thinking. This book attempts to take up this task. It does not pretend to be a definitive or finished analysis. Indeed, at most it is an initial and partial expression of a contemporary dialectical theology. It takes far too much for granted, and it never fully explores the questions it raises. Later work, I hope, will compensate for these deficiencies. Let it simply be said at this point that this book attempts to pose certain fundamental theological questions, and these questions are the product of a new and revolutionary historical situation. This situation can never be met by theological thinking which simply takes for granted premodern or prerevolutionary principles and categories. Thus far theology has only begun the task of asking questions about the meaning of faith in response to a new and revolutionary world. If this book does no more than raise a few such questions, and raise them coherently and consistently, it will have fulfilled its purpose. Finally, perhaps theology can only ask questions. If so, let it formulate questions which are already being asked, and asked by those who question most deeply in our world.

The questions posed by this book are the product of many years of theological wrestling, and while the form of the questions is my own, I believe that the questions themselves are shared by a wide community of inquirers. My first book, *Oriental Mysticism and Biblical Eschatology*, proceeded out of the conviction that the ground of the Christian faith had become invisible and unnamable in the modern world, and that the way back to this lost ground was to relate the foundations of ancient prophetic and primitive Christian faith to the higher and purer expressions of Oriental mysticism. This approach also entailed an opposition to and an attempted negation of the atheistic ground of the modern consciousness. But I soon realized that such a negation is illusory and impossible for anyone who accepts the reality of the modern consciousness and of modern history and society as well. Then the work of Mircea Eliade opened me to a deeper realization of the dialectical nature of the religious consciousness, and I wrote *Mircea Eliade and the Dialectic of the Sacred* in an attempt to unite Eliade's dialectical understanding of religion and Kierkegaard's dialectical understanding of faith. This book concludes with a theological analysis of Nietzsche's vision of Eternal Recurrence, which I continue to believe is the purest expression of modern atheism, and my analysis of Nietzsche's vision intended to demonstrate the dialectical identity of the most radical expressions of the sacred and the profane. By this route I was led to the imaginative vision of Blake and the dialectical method of Hegel, and I wrote *The New Apocalypse* with the conviction that genuine or total atheism is at once both profoundly Christian and the fundamental source of the modern consciousness and the modern world. Immediately after completing *The New Apocalypse,* I wrote *The Gospel of Christian Atheism,* hoping thereby to communicate both the meaning of radical faith and the Christian identity of modern atheism to the Christian reader. In one sense, *The Descent Into*

Hell is in continuity with my previous work, but in another sense it marks a new direction and a fresh voyage. For I am losing all sense of the particular identity of the Christian faith, and have become persuaded that Christ is actively and immediately present wherever darkness or Hell is actual and real.

A portion of the first chapter of this book was given as one in a series of lectures on revolution in the modern world at Southampton College, and a preliminary version of the last chapter was given as the Brewer Lectures in Comparative Religion at Beloit College. Much of the thinking that went into the book was evolved in response to questions and criticisms which I encountered on many campuses, and my deepest regret about the book is that it does so little justice to the penetrating questions and critiques which I have received from many quarters. While finishing the book I was also engaged in writing responses to a collection of theological critiques of my work edited by John B. Cobb, Jr., and these critiques too were a decisive factor in the writing of the book. John Cobb has been my most longstanding and my ablest theological critic, and I benefited immensely from his thinking during the years when this book was being conceived. I also was deeply challenged by a radical theological circle at Emory University, perhaps the one university in the country which supports radical theological thinking. I am also grateful to Claude B. McCaleb and Erik A. Langkjaer, both of whom have done so much for radical theological confrontation and publication during the past few years. But most of all I am grateful to my wife, Alma, who carefully read and criticized every page of the manuscript, and to whom the book is dedicated if only to indicate the most immediate source of whatever insight this descent into Hell may contain.

Thomas J. J. Altizer

Contents

✳

I

Faith
and
Revolution

*

1 ✳

Ours is a time in which the promise of a
new revolution appears to be everywhere about us, and
perhaps most so in the public arena of religion and faith;
yet our fundamental institutions and ideas, as witness our
churches and theologies, do not seem to be open to even
the possibility of far-reaching or radical change. Theologians and churchmen compete with one another in calling for a thoroughgoing transformation and translation of
our given words and gestures, our inherited religious
symbols and modes of speech, our forms of worship and
teaching, and our ecclesiastical organizations. But such
concern becomes all too easily not only a mask but also a
means of resolutely defending an underlying deposit of
faith and belief. A compulsion for relevance and the new
can in itself warn us of the presence of an attachment to
the irrelevant and the old. It can also be a means of deepening the power of an ancient symbol by disguising its
name. For an inherited and traditional faith can prolong

its life in a revolutionary situation by preserving itself inviolate from contact with life and experience, thereby isolating the inner reality of faith from the threat and the
challenge of the world which it confronts.

Then faith becomes invisible and inaudible, or unnamable and unseen in the world in which it exists, leading to
a situation in which faith can be neither attacked nor proclaimed, if only because its meaning and reality are confined to a hidden or esoteric realm. We should note,
moreover, that invisibility and inaudibility have been the
purest vehicles for the expression of the sacred. Silence
and emptiness have always been natural and inevitable
foundations of Eastern vision, for here religious vision
evolves and becomes real by way of negating and reversing the natural or given condition of consciousness and
experience. If everything which is manifest in the ordinary state of human experience is either a veil or an obstacle to the realization of true vision and liberation, then
all human activities must finally be emptied and silenced,
if full freedom or salvation is to become real. Thus when
contemporary Christian expressions of faith follow a way
of silence, either by turning the center of faith away from
exposure to the world or by refusing to speak the language of faith itself, they are following an ancient religious way, and one that could even be judged to be normative in the Orient. The simple fact that religious ways
of silence and emptiness have been given their highest
and most total expressions in the East—so much so that
their corresponding Western expressions all but pale into

insignificance by comparison—should give pause to the contemporary Christian who is tempted by this path.

Ironically enough, something like a way of silence now shows signs of becoming the dominant way of contemporary faith, and this in the name of revolution. Virtually all serious spokesmen for faith are now agreed that we are living in a new historical situation in which the traditional language of faith has become either archaic or unreal. Accordingly, the man of faith in our day is being driven to both an external and an internal silence. Not being able to speak the given or inherited language and symbols of faith, or, for that matter, to speak positively or affirmatively of faith, the man of faith is now choosing a negative way, a mode of attacking all existing or speakable symbols of faith. Once again iconoclasm is becoming the center of faith, and we must remind ourselves of the meaning of iconoclasm. Pure iconoclasm is a negation of all human expressions of faith; it speaks against all cultural, social, and historical ideas and images of belief. Nevertheless, it appears in many forms, and it performs two essential although differing functions. On the one hand, it can negate an existing form of religion so as to make possible the advent of a new form of faith or praxis, as can be seen not only in the Old Testament and the Koran but also in Buddhism and Taoism. On the other hand, it can serve as a defensive measure against an alien and threatening attraction, whether of a positive or negative kind. In this form, iconoclasm has played a major role in all of the monotheistic religious traditions originat-

ing in the Near East, and even the biblical prophets employed iconoclasm as a way of resisting and opposing the
higher cultural world of the ancient Near East.

Consequently, iconoclasm can be a way of either moving forward to a new or purer form of faith or of resisting
an alien consciousness and experience so as to make possible the preservation and continual identity of an ancient
or original form of faith. No doubt a line between the two
can never clearly be drawn, but we should be aware of
the fact that iconoclasm can be a means of opposing the
forward movement of history. True iconoclasm can be either revolutionary or counterrevolutionary, either an indispensable presupposition for a leap ahead of consciousness or a retreat to an earlier historical era or mode of
consciousness. But to speak in this manner of revolution
and counterrevolution is to speak from a Western point of
view, and from a modern Western point of view at that.
In an Eastern context, a retreat to an earlier mode of consciousness can be understood as a return to a prehistoric
or preconscious humanity. Here, the apparent and given
forms of consciousness are identified as lower or illusory
forms of an unfallen and undifferentiated consciousness, a
total consciousness which is all-inclusive and all-compre-
hending, and whose veiling or stilling brings about the
advent of pain and illusion. What the West knows as the
backward movement of regression, the East can name as
the forward movement of progression and liberation, as
the reversal of ignorance and suffering, and the release of
freedom and calm. From an Eastern point of view, it is

the advent of motion and division, of a differentiated consciousness and its corresponding expression, a world or
cosmos appearing in the form of movement and process,
which is the ultimate source of all ignorance and pain.
Only a stilling of the source of movement and differentia-
tion can lead to that final liberation which Eastern vision
knows as truth.

Hence it is not accidental that the East is once again
exercising such a powerful religious fascination upon the
West. If the foundations of everything which the West
has known as truth and order appear to be coming to an
end, or if, at the very least, what the West has consciously known and historically experienced as religious
or ultimate truth is in a state of near-collapse or self-dis-
solution, then an Eastern way must appear all the more
powerful in the West, if only because it becomes manifest
to us as the dissolution of all which we have known as
reality and truth. The very alien quality of Eastern ways
—their immense distance from what we can humanly
know and experience as faith—has since the Enlightenment given the East a new and vital image, particularly
insofar as it calls for a reversal of what the West has
known as knowledge and action. Not only has the East
gained a new power for us, but its dissolution of the ultimate ground of motion and process has been given a new
expression in the West. So it is that the most advanced
forms of the imagination in the West are now assaulting
all form and structure and attempting in their own manner to dissolve everything which has appeared in the

dominant life of the West as selfhood and self-consciousness, if only because all we have known as life is now appearing in the image of impotence and death.

Western ways of faith are also finding their own routes
to Eastern ways, and most effectively so through their
iconoclastic attacks upon religion. All too obviously Western forms of religion have become inadequate to bear the
burdens now placed upon them, and in an historical situation of crisis and transition, their very bondage to our
historical past has alienated them from the realities of the
present. Iconoclasm becomes all the more attractive if the
religion it attacks appears to be archaic and unreal. It is
Western historical forms of religion which are now under
heaviest attack from the modern Christian spokesmen of
faith, but, interestingly enough, these are attacked not
because they are past or irrelevant, but rather because
they are expressions of religion. When religion is understood as a social and cultural embodiment of the quest for
the sacred, or as a sinful or illusory quest for an unrealiz-
able infinite or beyond, then religion can be attacked as a
barrier to faith, and iconoclasm can be a way to the recovery and renewal of faith. Just as Eastern visionaries
call for a reversal of history and consciousness, Western
theologians are now calling for a reversal of the specifically Western movement of history, which is here understood as embodying a fall from an original or primitive
Christianity to an historical or Western Christendom.
The initial movement of Christianity from its original and
presumably biblical form to a new cultural and historical

expression then becomes condemned as a betrayal of faith itself, and as a reversal of revelation. But who can fail to note that the theologian who identifies faith with its original expression, and condemns every subsequent historical movement of faith, except those attempting to return to the Bible, is unknowingly reflecting those Eastern conceptions of ultimate truth which identify truth with its primordial and prehistoric expressions?

Even Roman Catholic theologians are now calling for a return to the Bible, thereby joining their orthodox Protestant brethren, who have long called for a reversal of our history and a return to a prehistoric or pre-Western biblical faith and innocence. Nor are theologians or churchmen so naïve as they are often presumed to be. Genuine calls for a return to the Bible are inevitably accompanied by violent assaults upon all the history that succeeds the Bible, thus revealing not only their counterrevolutionary identity but also their profound opposition to the reality and movement of history. Indeed, at this point, we can reach one essential meaning of a counterrevolutionary theology and faith. The fundamental problem at hand is that the movement of Western history is manifestly a movement away from what is openly or publicly identifiable to the Christian as faith. Insofar as the Christian identifies faith with either its biblical or its ecclesiastical symbols, it is clear beyond doubt that the social, the cultural, and the interior human worlds which we confront are radically estranged from faith, and this estrangement is obviously the product of a long and continuous historical process. Therefore the Christian who identifies the essence of faith with its past or original expressions, and who chooses to attempt to exist in faith, must either set himself against what is manifest as the reality and movement of history, or must choose a form of faith which is isolated from and unaffected by everything which appears and is real as the movement and process of history.

Iconoclasm can serve either choice, for its assault upon every human expression of a quest for the ultimate can serve as an attack upon either the secularizing movement of Western history or upon any social or cultural expression which demands an ultimate loyalty or commitment. Both are rejected in the name of the integral limits of consciousness and experience, and hence neither can offer an ultimate challenge to faith. Nevertheless, in our situation, iconoclastic attacks upon a secular culture and society serve to isolate faith from history. This is so because the secular momentum of Western society and culture has long since reached such a point as to eclipse and annul the social and cultural expressions of faith; the new world which has established itself in our history is a world which has wholly detached itself from the traditional faith of Christendom, and the Christian who exists in this world must risk an ultimate loss of faith. It is the actuality of a new historical situation in which faith confronts a human world which is totally alienated from itself that impels faith to a new and radical iconoclastic assault upon that world if only as a means of existing in its presence. Whether or not all men now live in a crisis situation, the Christian inevitably does so; the particular nature of our crisis has already led the most passionate men of faith to an absolute opposition to our history, and now threatens to lead all who would live in the Christian faith in our world to an ultimate attempt to escape history.

II ✳

Fortunately, our situation continues to be an open one, and to contain within itself the potentiality for diverse paths of resolution, but it is incumbent upon us to understand those forces which would lead us to regression and retreat. If the Christian faith is finally forced to judge that the modern world is antithetically related to faith, or that the forward moving currents of society and consciousness are leading to the total dissolution of faith, then Christianity can only choose a counterrevolutionary course of opposing the dominant movement of our history. Or, if Christianity is truly to embrace our world and its revolutionary momentum, it must be prepared to embrace an historical movement reversing and annulling all previously established historical forms of faith. This challenge would appear to be all too obvious, but it continues to be unanswered by modern theology. What one finds in the most influential expressions of modern Christian theology is the attempt to isolate history from faith in such a manner as to make history neutral in the presence of faith. Theological attempts to evolve a purely existential or solitary form of faith obviously seek to isolate faith from history, and in effect negate history as the arena of faith. Despite appearances to the contrary, neither theologies of "secularization" nor theologies of "hope" truly affirm the modern world. For the one embraces the progressive historical dissolution of religion in the West only as a means of radically distinguishing the center of faith from the center of the world, and the other directs faith away from the historical present to a distant and utopian future, and a future which can become real for faith only when it is linked with the traditional and archaic symbol of the resurrection. In a parallel manner, the new scholasticism of Catholic theology can promise a reconciliation of faith with the contemporary world only by way of abandoning or reversing the whole movement of postmedieval history. Throughout all these movements of modern theology, and in others as well, we may observe the continual attempt to establish the truth and reality of faith by way of detaching and isolating faith from what is manifest as the actual movement and reality of our history.

Does this mean that the contemporary Christian can accept the modern world only insofar as he succeeds in establishing an impassable barrier between the world and faith? Can the Christian finally accept and affirm the full movement of history only insofar as it is totally isolated from faith? Is Christianity, then, despite the all but unanimous theological claims to the contrary, a nonhistorical form of faith? Theologically considered, the problem can be simply stated as the classical problem of dualism, the problem of whether or not Christianity finally has a dualistic ground. This problem has been evaded by most modern theology by the simple tactic of giving dualism a new name and face. For the most part this is done by establishing such a radical gulf between the world and faith that neither can be judged in terms of the other, and each can only stand and appear in its own inherent form and light. Thereby, it is claimed, religious or classical theological dualism is transcended by virtue of the fact that here neither faith nor the world opposes the other, and each is manifest in such a way as to take its meaning solely from itself. Indeed, the claim can then be made that it is precisely when faith is most truly itself that the world can stand and appear autonomously by being freed of all dependence upon faith. So likewise faith can then exist in a new freedom wherein it transcends all possibility of threat or opposition from the world.

But is it truly possible so to dissociate faith and history, or the world and faith, that neither will oppose the other, but that, on the contrary, each will support and affirm the other by most fully being itself? If this were so, then the Christian could look upon the anti-Christian expressions of the modern world as a temporary and passing phenomenon, and one even now being replaced by a new secularism which is either neutral or indifferent to faith. Can there truly be a form of Christianity which is indifferent to the presence before and about it of a fully secular or radically profane world? Has modern theology in fact accepted the autonomy of the modern world? Surely the

answer to this question can only be no. For where in
modern theology can one find an acceptance of the world
in its own terms? On the contrary, do we not far rather
find that theology can accept an autonomous world only
by stripping it of every ultimate meaning and value,
thereby making it finally dependent upon faith? By this
means, a seemingly new theology incorporates a classical
theological dualism: for it can maintain the reality and
truth of faith only by denying the ultimate meaning and
life of the world.

Once a subjective and interior realm is chosen as the
arena of faith, and this arena is disjoined and isolated
from the public or historical arena of consciousness and
experience, then only insofar as the historical arena is
given but a guarded or secondary loyalty and commitment can the interior realm be preserved as the center of
ultimate loyalty and faith. Accordingly, theologies so isolating faith from history embrace the goal of secularizing
or desanctifying all forms of consciousness and society.
History itself must be desanctified, or stripped of all ultimate meaning and identity, if only to make possible the
preservation of faith. All social and cultural expressions of
life must then be objectified, or purged of any true
subjective or interior meaning, and this means that the
autonomous expressions of consciousness and experience
must be dehumanized so that they can in no sense im-
pinge upon the autonomy of faith. Thus theological or ecclesiastical calls for secularization or desanctification cannot be limited to the social and political realms; no

expression of culture or consciousness is allowed to claim a final or ultimate loyalty, as every human voice is finally stilled in the presence of the demand of faith.

One decisive mark of the modern world is its will to break or transcend all previous limits placed upon the condition of man and society. While this will or impulse or movement is present in virtually all expressions of modern life, it is perhaps most openly manifest in the religious sphere, where the traditional Christian idea of God as the absolutely sovereign and transcendent Lord has been assaulted as an ultimate barrier to the expansion of consciousness and experience. At no other point has the whole movement of modern history seemed to be more anti-Christian, particularly insofar as modern theologians have seized upon the Old Testament symbol of the creatureliness of man and the world as the most decisive ground of the Christian faith. Whereas the traditional language of faith speaks of the ultimate reality of God and eternity and the provisional and subordinate reality of man and the world, the modern consciousness has abandoned and negated every such distinction and transformed the traditional quest for transcendence into a new and radical quest for an eternity or infinity which is pure immanence, which is present here and now in our world and experience or not truly present or real at all. In response to this quest, modern Christian theological spokesmen for faith have demanded that consciousness and experience be limited and enclosed by the authority of God and His Word, and human history be understood as being confined to a finite or at most penultimate arena and identity. But to affirm the creatureliness or finitude of man and the world, and to seek to impose limits or barriers upon the infinite expansion of consciousness and experience, is to speak against the whole movement of modern history, and to make faith antithetical to everything which is manifest as reality in the modern world.

Thus the believer who chooses to isolate faith from history is finally driven to an opposition to history, to a desperate effort to reverse the historical processes leading to the modern world, to the frightful necessity of stilling or dissolving the deepest expressions of modern life and consciousness. It is precisely such a situation which has led to a veiling of the meaning of faith, to the silence of the most sophisticated spokesmen for faith, and above all to a moratorium upon all theological language about God. A glance at the contemporary theological situation illuminates this problem. For here we find either a biblical theology elucidating the meaning of God in ancient biblical language, or a scholastic theology continuing to formulate the meaning of God in premodern concepts and ideas, or a philosophical theology attempting to construct a purely abstract and hence finally nontheological conception of God, or diverse forms of theology either directing theology away from the question of God or repudiating all language about God whatsoever. What one fails to find in modern theology is a serious or disciplined attempt to link or unite a biblical or premodern conception or symbol of God with the meaning of God or the infinite or the ultimate in contemporary consciousness and experience. Only by preserving the name of God inviolate from the reality of modern history and life can the man of faith continue to speak the name of God. Only by attacking every modern meaning of God or the sacred or the ultimate can faith preserve its given identity, or exist in continuity with its ancient or original face.

Our situation is such that even to attempt to speak the name of God, with a genuine and a human voice, is to engage in either a revolutionary or a counterrevolutionary act. Moreover, an examination of the very attempt to speak the name of God can unveil the religious or theological meaning of revolution and counterrevolution: the one an act of transforming a primary given so as to make it active and real in the present, and the other an act of stilling or reversing the present so as to make it open to a lost or forgotten original ground. When a seemingly unbridgeable chasm exists between an original center or ground and its present embodiment or manifestation—and this is a fundamental meaning of modern symbols of the absence or the silence or the death of God—then any attempt to reach that ground must inevitably be of a radical nature, and all genuine forms of theology, whether of a revolutionary or counterrevolutionary nature, will inescapably be cast in a radical mold. The very fact that theology has reversed its apparent or former identity and become for us a radical quest is compelling evidence of the theological truth that the meaning of God is inseparable and finally indistinguishable from its human or historical embodiment. When God is silent or hidden or absent, the very meaning of God vanishes from consciousness, and the name of God evokes a vanishing echo, a gnawing numbness, or a void.

One of the bitterest truths which we have been forced to learn is that all language is human language, even including language about God, and human language, as opposed to a divine or angelic language, is empty and meaningless when it evokes no response, and thus ceases to be language when it is no longer capable of being the instrument of communication or expression. No longer is it possible to believe that a sacred, a revealed, or a biblical language stands autonomously on its own ground, being in no need of a human or an historical expression. Therefore we also no longer believe that any language whatsoever, including the symbolic language of faith, can contain any genuine meaning which cannot be given a human expression. Not only is a language which cannot be embodied in consciousness and experience no language at all, but it contains no meaning, and must be judged to be a meaningless cipher or surd. True, a language may have a restricted, a limited, a partial, or an ambivalent meaning, or, for that matter, a paradoxical or nihilistic meaning, but meaning it has and this to the extent that it can truly be judged to be language. All of these strictures apply to language about God, even including that language spoken in faith about God, and thus the man of faith has been forced to recognize that when the language of faith is not spoken faith itself recedes and disappears. But if faith must speak, must it speak in the language at hand? Must it speak in the language which is peculiar or distinctive to the particular historical moment in which it lives? Or can it speak about a God who is universally present and who can be truly evoked only by a language transcending every particular or contingent mode of expression?

Not the least of the many gifts bequeathed us by the modern era is the realization that what we know as God is not a universal datum in human experience but is rather the product of a particular historical tradition. The attempt to speak of deity or the divine as a universal in language and consciousness breaks down when it confronts historical traditions far removed from its own. We have discovered not only that the Orient knows little or nothing of what the West has known as God, but also that the meaning of deity in ancient Greece and Rome is almost wholly incompatible with the meaning of God in Christendom, to say nothing of the fact that it simply is not possible to translate into Christian theological language what the Muslim or the Jew knows as God. Just as the idea of a universal humanity is an abstract chimera, and one that reduces the actual man to an inhuman or subhuman level, so likewise an abstract and universal idea of God can be reached only by negating and dissolving that meaning of God which is manifest in consciousness and experience. Nor is it possible for us actually to know or name a deity who can stand or appear autonomously, or be enclosed within itself. Otherwise, deity could not be present to consciousness. Or, it could be present to no consciousness but its own; nor could it be susceptible to imagery or speech. Theologically stated, we could say that there is no God but the revealed God; the unrevealed God is nothing at all. Or, to make the same point in another context, the only God about whom we can speak is the God who is manifest in consciousness and real in experience. Therefore the God whom we can name is the God who is actualized or realized in history, the God whom our history has given us. Apart from history, God is not only unrealized but unreal: hence any attempt to transcend history in speaking about God must culminate in total silence.

Why, then, it may well be asked, should one attempt to speak about God? Should not silence about God be the way not only of wisdom but also of faith? Do we not invariably fall not only into foolishness but also into blasphemy in all our efforts to speak about God? Let it first be said that whoever has been given the name of God can refuse to speak about God only with grave danger to himself. If one has been given a history in which God is present, then one must respond, whether positively or negatively, or both, to the name of God, if only as a means of making one's history one's own. If all those who ignore history become its victims, then it should also be realized that whoever ignores the God of our history becomes the victim of God. Or, rather, he becomes the passive if unconscious prisoner of those forms of consciousness and experience which have named and embodied God. To speak of God is to speak of that which has been and is present as God, which has been given us as God, and which we can ignore only at the cost of turning away from ourselves. The only God about whom we can actually speak is the "given" God, the God who is real only inasmuch as He is or has been present and actual to us. Even if we are alienated from the God of our history, God is real in our very alienation, and we must speak His name to name ourselves. For the God whom we have been given has "named" Himself in us, and named Himself in such a manner that we cannot dissociate His identity from our own. There can be no speech about a God who is eternally Wholly Other, no image or symbol of a God who is wholly transcendent and apart, no vision or understanding of a God who exists only in Himself. Thus to speak about God is not simply to speak about an "other," it is also to speak about ourselves, about that which is or has been actual and real to us.

III ✳

This is not to say that we can truly speak about God in speaking about that which is immediately or apparently given to us. The God whom we have been given is a God lying beyond our ordinary consciousness, a God apart from our common experience. Nevertheless, all those who inherit the Christian horizon of faith have been given a God who has named or revealed Himself in Christ as having fully and totally given Himself to us. The Christian knows a God who has fully and finally revealed Himself in Christ, and the Christ in whom God is most fully revealed is not a distant and transcendent Lord, but is rather the Word made flesh, the Lamb and the Shepherd who is the source of forgiveness and life, the bearer of the glad tidings of the advent of a new time of total joy and celebration. Christ is the Christian name of the God who is totally for us and with us, and the Christ whom the Christian has been given is present in the fullness of the world and time, at the center of flesh and consciousness. Thus Christ is also the Christian name for the fullness of life and the world, for the total expansion of consciousness and experience. Insofar as consciousness or experience is active and real it bears the impress of what the Christian has been given in Christ, for the Christian confesses the Christ who is present wherever life and experience are most active and real.

Accordingly, the Christian, and all who inherit or have been given the Christian God, know a God whose name and identity is present wherever there is a fullness of consciousness. This is not to say that the Christian name of God is explicitly or openly manifest in the activity of consciousness, but it is to say that wherever consciousness realizes or unfolds itself it gives witness to the God whom the Christian knows as being not vicariously but rather actually present in Christ. The Christian has been given the God who in Christ is the source of the expansion and evolution of consciousness, and even though the form and image of God may not be openly present in the movement of consciousness, the Christian is bound to that totally given God who is present even in His apparent absence from consciousness and life. The God whom the Christian knows and confesses can never truly be absent from the fullness of life and the world: it is rather consciousness and experience which must be judged by the Christian to be partial and fragmentary when they fail to give witness to God. Indeed, it is above all the Christian consciousness which must be judged to be empty and unreal when it fails to embody or make actual and manifest the God who has totally given Himself to us in Christ.

Our theological dilemma derives from the fact that there seems to be no way from the actuality of contemporary consciousness and experience to the God who has made Himself actual and manifest in Christ as being for us and with us in life and the world. True, the theologian can resolve this dilemma by so conceiving the reality of God and the world as to establish an absolute hiatus between them, either by conceiving each as the antithesis of the other, or by dualistically isolating the center of faith from the actuality and immediacy of life in the world. But to follow such a path is to refuse the God who is the ground of our history, the God whom the Christian faith proclaims to be the center of history and consciousness, the alpha and omega of history and the world. Ironically, theologies attempting to speak in the name of the orthodox Christian conception of the absolute sovereignty and transcendence of God can now speak only by negating their own foundation, only by reversing the uniquely

Christian name and identity of the God who is fully present and real in Christ. For to proclaim a God who is unknowable in our history, or silent and invisible in our experience, is to say no to the God who has actually become incarnate in the world, embodying Himself at the center of
history and life.

If the God who is uniquely present in the Christian
faith is the God who appears and is real at the center of
consciousness, who is present not in the emptiness but
rather in the fullness of life and the world, then it is not
the Christian God who hides Himself in the depths of the
unconscious, or who is manifest only at the limits and
boundaries of human experience. It is far rather Christian
efforts to negate and escape the God who has fully given
Himself to us in Christ which has resulted in Christian
conceptions of an impassably distant and alien God, a
God who is infinitely removed from man and the world,
and whose Word can be heard and obeyed only by a broken and impotent humanity. If the only God whom the
Christian can actually name today is a God who is infinitely distant and apart, then all too naturally the theologian will be silent about God, and will give himself instead to claiming for God a world which shows no signs
of His presence. Or, rather, from the point of view of the
dominant theological conception of God in our century, it
is precisely a godless world which most deeply witnesses
to the presence of faith. For true faith strips the world of
the presence of the divine, renouncing every illusory conception or image of the actual presence of the infinite in

the finite, allowing the world to stand forth in its totally creaturely identity. Then not only can our world be claimed for God, and claimed for the God who is totally absent from the world, but the whole historical process of secularization in the West can be claimed as the deepest witness to the promise and identity of the biblical God. Here, we behold the further irony of theologians who not only delight in atheism and secularism in the name of Christian orthodoxy, but who employ a celebration of the secular, both the secular society and the secular consciousness, as a means of upholding and preserving obedience to the God of Christian orthodoxy. Are we to believe that it is only insofar as God is banished from consciousness and experience that the God of the Christian tradition can now be present in faith?

Or can we turn to theological liberalism or modernism for a reconception of God, a new understanding of God which may make possible for the Christian a recognition of the presence of God in our world? Liberalism in theology, however, just as liberalism in political theory, is inextricably bound to a premodern or precontemporary theoretical structure, a structure postulating a fundamental harmony in the world, an ultimate coherence between all the parts or dimensions or faces of the real. Then God is named as the source of that harmony, the ground of a universal truth, the origin of a cosmic order. Fortunately or unfortunately, no such harmony or order is now manifest in the world, whether interiorly or exteriorly, and the search for the ground of a lost harmony is a counterrevolutionary act, an attempt to reverse all the history that follows upon the advent of the modern world. Nor can theological or religious liberalism meet the human situation of the contemporary world, a situation in which the name of God has become unspeakable as the source or image of energy and life. For we are not simply mute in the presence of the name of God, we are also driven to rebellion and defiance: a defiance arising from our inability to dissociate the very name of God as we have been given it from an historical era that is past, and since we know that that era is fully past, it can only appear as unreal and lifeless to us insofar as it is evoked or remembered in the present. It is significant that the idea of the radical or total transcendence of God was not established at the center of religious thinking until the nineteenth century. Moreover, it was so established by prophetic thinkers such as Kierkegaard and Dostoyevsky who understood the theological significance of our new and revolutionary situation, a situation before which theological liberalism has all but collapsed.

Dare we then accept the persistent calls about us for a new honesty of faith? Can we be honest to God without being dishonest to faith? Can we affirm what is humanly namable as God without denying what we have been given as the God of faith? To pose these questions is to recognize that our choice is not simply one of being faithful or unfaithful to the God whom we have been given. It is rather one of either affirming the God who is now namable by faith or repudiating that God in the name of the

God whom we could once know in faith. Or, more fully stated, a contemporary Christian attempt to speak the name of God must engage in either a revolutionary assault upon everything about and within us which is manifest as consciousness, experience, and speech, or an equally revolutionary assault upon everything which is now manifest to faith as the meaning and reality of God. If the latter course is chosen we must embrace the paradox of opposing and negating the very name of God in response to a uniquely Christian faith and promise. Nor may the Christian continue to evade the demand that he speak the name of God. Silence and irresolution are luxuries which we can no longer afford, if we ever could, for faith will atrophy and perish if it is neither spoken nor unveiled. Once again the demand for decision is before us: we must decide how to act and speak in faith in our world. Moreover, the choice has very nearly already been made for us. The only theologies having genuine power today are all too clearly of a counterrevolutionary nature, even when they disguise their ground by speaking in the name of secularization or the future, or when they ease our conscience if not our minds by speaking the rhetoric of cultural or social or political revolution. No, we need not take seriously the theologian who speaks only about cultural or political revolution, unless we are interested in the impact of theology upon the churches. Rather, it is religious or theological revolution which is the domain of the theologian. In truth, both the theologian and the believer are now being driven to a revolutionary way, and the mere fact that even the attempts to formulate a revolutionary theology have thus far been both weak and fragmentary all but seals for many the counterrevolutionary identity of both theology and faith.

IV ✳

Is it true that theology, of necessity, must set itself against the forward-moving currents of the modern world? If a revolutionary theology is impossible, how is it that the prophetic and eschatological traditions of the Bible can appear even to us to be revolutionary, to say nothing of the proclamation of Jesus? We know that the reform prophets of the Old Testament not only opposed the dominant power of the world which they confronted but also succeeded in effecting a revolutionary transformation of the religious traditions of Israel. While the proclamation of Jesus may not initially appear to be revolutionary, and is not revolutionary in a strictly political sense, not even as revolutionary as was the message of the prophets which preceded it, it nevertheless is profoundly revolutionary in terms of the radical demand it places upon its hearers. But are these revolutionary motifs of the Bible of necessity stilled and muted when they are given a theological expression? Must theology invariably perform a conservative role inasmuch as its formulations serve to buttress and sanction an established community of faith? Is the very practice of theology inevitably an expression of those forces which must quiet or reverse the forward-moving currents of consciousness and society? Must theology be wholly identified with its priestly function, with its ecclesiastical role of conserving and preserving faith, or its social role of sanctioning all established institutions?

To accept such an identity of theology is to posit an antithetical relation between theology and its prophetic roots, or perhaps even to think of theology as a primary means whereby society resists and opposes all prophetic and revolutionary challenges. It also comes dangerously close either to denying that thinking can embody revolution or to asserting that a revolutionary faith can never be given a theoretical or conceptual meaning. And to skirt this danger is to face the choice of identifying revolution either as an opposition to the specific movement and forms of Western history or as pure anarchism. No doubt a great many today are making such a choice, and the reasons for doing so at times seem overwhelming. Nonetheless the truth must be faced that the consequence of refusing to identify revolution as a forward if radical historical movement is that revolution will be confined either to a sectarian elite standing outside of the great body of society or to an esoteric realm transcending the common and universal life of humanity. It would seem that neither alternative is open to the Christian believer, and therefore we must face the challenge of either seeking a revolutionary meaning of faith or of renouncing the very possibility of a revolutionary form of faith.

The vast majority of theologians, not even to speak of

ecclesiastical spokesmen, have conceived of faith,
whether openly or covertly, in such a manner as to make
it unthinkable as a revolutionary act or commitment. In
part this identification of faith as a nonrevolutionary
choice has been made in response to the reality of modern revolution. For all modern revolutions have been either openly and violently anti-Christian or directed
against the established power and forms of Christianity.
Genuine revolutions must oppose the religious forms and
forces they meet, if only because these are inevitably
rooted in the past, and revolutions by necessity must di-
rect themselves to uprooting and transforming the present
insofar as it is bound to the past. As opposed to anarchistic
and sectarian movements, modern revolutions have identified themselves with the forward movement of history.
Moreover, they have profoundly differed from the liberal
movements which they opposed by denying the classical
liberal thesis that history moves forward in a continuous
and unbroken manner. Instead, they have insisted that existing forms of consciousness and society make way for new
forms only by coming to their own end or dissolution. For a
genuinely new life and energy is never simply a fulfillment
or an organic outgrowth of the life which it succeeds or re-
places, if only because its radical newness can be born
only by way of the death of the body or form from which
it arises. In the name of a new life upon our future horizon,
the revolutionary wills the death of the totality of the past,
not with a nihilistic hatred of all historical forms of society
and consciousness, but rather with the conviction that the

true life of the past can reach its own realization only by bursting and transcending the forms in which it has been contained, once these cease to be open to the future.

A revolutionary situation is one in which the established or dominant forms of society and consciousness are fundamentally closed to the future and can preserve themselves only by compulsively returning to the past, a past which then appears in a dead or archaic form because in this situation it can offer no way into the future. But is this not exactly the situation of Christianity in the modern world? Is it any wonder that Christians today acknowledge that Christendom has perished, and that our theologians have all but forsaken the quest for the lost time of a living and vital Christian past? What useful purpose can be served, then, by looking for a revolutionary form of faith? Is it not true that faith is simply faith, wholly given in the past, and by no possibility open to a future which negates the past? But have we not learned again and again in our century that a prophetic and eschatological faith is directed wholly towards the future? Or is directed towards the present only insofar as the present bears the impact of a new and radical future? A truly eschatological future, so far from being a culmination or organic fulfillment of the past, can become manifest and real only by shattering or bringing to a final end everything which is rooted in the past. Can we not say then that an eschatological future can truly appear only in a revolutionary situation?

Christians have long claimed that Jesus appeared in a

revolutionary situation. Furthermore, it is unquestionably true that it was an eschatological form of faith which appeared in Jesus' proclamation. But is it not obvious that everything which is manifest today as Christianity and the church is a form of society and consciousness deeply rooted in the past? In one sense, at least, it is even possible to say that Christianity and Christendom are more profoundly rooted in the past than any other form of religion or culture. Christianity and Christendom, in establishing their dominant social and cultural forms, did not simply accept or sanction the historical past lying behind them. Each and both together created a new sacred history of the past, a past unknown to the ancient Greek or Jew or Roman, but which now for the first time was unveiled as the anticipation or forerunner of a Christian world. It is important to note that no other cultural world or empire, neither in the Far nor the Near East, created or recreated a total historical past as a preparation and justification for itself. Nor did any other cultural or religious world, including even ancient Israel, create an idea of history or providence wherein every human or historical event is sustained and directed by an omniscient and redemptive God. Indeed, nowhere else in history do we find a form of consciousness so comprehensively and pervasively grounded in a deity who appears as the God of the past, the Creator whose original and absolute power is the sole source of all meaning and life.

Has the Christian taken with sufficient seriousness the extent to which he identifies God as the Creator? Must not the Christian who so identifies God inevitably be rooted in the past, not simply in an historical past, debilitating as this is in a revolutionary age, but more deeply in a cosmic past? That is to say a past which is the absolute point of our beginning, wherefrom our deepest identity derives? Does not such an identity strengthen and sanction all those regressive impulses within us which strive to return not simply to an original innocence but also to a primordial or original condition of existence? If our truest nature is that originally given us by the Creator, must we not then embrace an end which is our beginning, a goal which is our advent or birth? What could more deeply set us against a genuine future than a bondage to the God who appears to consciousness in the form of the Creator? Is it not inevitable that a faith grounded in this form of deity must assume a counterrevolutionary form, directing itself against every call from the future? And is there any other point at which we can so decisively perceive the gulf dividing the Christian world today from the eschatological proclamation of Jesus? Must we not finally confess that it is now our Christian faith in God which most deeply turns us away from the call and reality of Christ?

Before daring to face such questions it is imperative that we recognize that a truly eschatological faith is not simply directed toward the future, or toward any future lying at hand. On the contrary, it is directed to that future, and that future alone, which can be realized only by way of a total uprooting of the present. Everything in the present which is grounded in the past must be transformed, and totally transformed at that. Therefore a fully eschatological faith proclaims an absolute end of all which appears and is real in the form of the past. Once granted that an eschatological faith can only be so defined, or only so defined by us, then will it not become ever more apparent that the God who is manifest in the Christian world today is the antithesis of the Kingdom of God proclaimed by Jesus? Is not the new totality proclaimed by Jesus a new totality which breaks into the present from the future? This simple fact has overwhelming theological implications, not the least of them being that to the extent that faith embodies and reflects the past it will be closed to the new totality at hand. Moreover, to the extent that faith is bound to a deity appearing to consciousness in the form of the past, or appearing as the primordial Creator, it will be closed to a Kingdom of God appearing from the future. None of these crucial theological points can be explored at this juncture of our analysis, but posing them can lead us to ask if the God who gradually but ever more comprehensively evolved in the church and Christendom is the reversal of the Kingdom of God which Jesus proclaimed.

By this path, too, we can understand the irony deriving from the fact that the line between revolutionary and counterrevolutionary thinking is so subtle or elusive in modern theology. Already, beginning with Pascal, the great defenders of faith in the modern world have been forced to rebel not only against the most powerful expressions of the modern consciousness but also against those movements of consciousness and society most decisively leading to the modern era. Once faith encountered a world whose very foundations were opposed to the God of faith, it became necessary not only to challenge those foundations but also to unravel and even reverse all those forces and movements leading to the present form and power of the world. Seeds of unbelief were discovered and unearthed not only in secular consciousness and society but also in religious and theological movements, particularly insofar as these were apprehended as moving away from the original foundations of faith. Under the impact of this kind of radical analysis, the breech between the modern form of Christendom and the church and its biblical foundation had so widened that, with Kierkegaard, it became necessary to oppose and reverse all the history that lies between the New Testament and the present. Thus the very necessity for faith of reversing the ever-increasing dissolution of faith in the Christian world led not only to a counterrevolutionary attack upon the modern world but also to a revolutionary assault upon the whole historical movement of Christianity. Kierkegaard discovered a radically new understanding of faith by negating and reversing the history of Christendom and the church. Twentieth century neo-orthodox theology, however, while initially embracing Kierkegaard's discovery, was progressively forced by its loyalty to the authority of the church to numb and disguise a radical understanding of faith. Hence it finally fell back upon an absolute distinction between the church and Christendom, and a dualistic isolation of the history of faith from the historical movements of consciousness and society.

We can see in this pattern, however, that a theological thinking which is forced by faith itself to rebel against the modern movement of history can play a revolutionary role inasmuch as it is led to negate and reverse the history of the church or the history of faith. Only when theology chooses to stand firmly upon an inherited ecclesiastical form of faith, taking as its foundation the established and dominant symbols of faith, is it forced into a fully counterrevolutionary path. Such a path leads it not only to a total resistance to every revolutionary attack upon the Christian consciousness and society, but also to a role of sanctioning the whole movement of Christian history, including the original movement from an eschatological to a noneschatological form of faith. From our present vantage point, this initial historical movement from a prophetic and eschatological faith to a priestly and ecclesiastical faith is the most revolutionary or counterrevolutionary event in the history of Christianity. So it is that we are treated to the further irony of the great revolutionaries of the modern world—such as Hegel, Marx, and Nietzsche—employing the eschatological forms and imagery of New Testament faith, as well as its Old Testament prophetic counterpart, as their most powerful weapons against the theological defenders of a dying Christian world. Today it is Christian theologians who must learn the meaning of a radical escha-

tological faith from seemingly anti-Christian revolutionaries!

For these modern revolutionaries have taught us the
eschatological truth that a new world or future can become real only by way of a total negation and reversal of
the world of the past. True revolution is not simply an
opening to the future but also a closing of the past. Yet
the past which is negated by a revolutionary future cannot simply be negated or forgotten. It must be transcended by way of a reversal of the past, a reversal bringing a totally new light and meaning to everything which
is manifest as the past, and therefore a reversal fully
transforming the whole horizon of the present. Modern
revolutionary assaults upon the whole movement of a profane or secular history can now serve not only as models
but also as sources for a revolutionary theological assault
upon the history of faith. Indeed, such an assault has already occurred in revolutionary thinking, and not only in
the apparently anti-Christian thinking of Hegel, Marx,
and Nietzsche, but also in the manifestly Christian thinking of Blake, Kierkegaard, and Dostoyevsky. Already
these thinkers have forged a path which promises to lead
to a full understanding of how the whole history of faith
can betray and reverse itself. Perhaps thereby we shall
come to see not only how the Christian God has evolved
into the opposite of his original identity, but also how the
Christian God now embodies in a reverse form his original promise and life.

V ✳

If a genuine dialectical understanding of such a reverse movement of faith has already been given us in the prophetic thinkers of the nineteenth century, then the theological task before us is the enormous one of appropriating such a way of thinking so as to make meaningful to a community of faith the inversion or reversal in our history of the meaning and reality of God. Only an understanding of how the vacuous and infinitely distant God who is now manifest to consciousness and experience is the opposite of the Kingdom of God which Jesus proclaimed and enacted, can make possible a Christian assault upon that faith in God which is the source of our deepest bondage to the past. Not only will the Christian thereby become open to a revolutionary future but he will discover in that future a rebirth of a long-lost or hidden eschatological faith. The fact that the Christian inherits a history in which God is manifest as being totally for us and with us—as witness Jesus' triumphant announcement of the dawning of the Kingdom of God—can prepare us for a radical opposition to a purely transcendent and alien God. Such opposition will lead us to a recognition that the God who is silent and apart, or invisible and solitary, or unspeakable and unnamable in any tongue is a God who is not simply other than the Kingdom of God which Jesus proclaimed but is Himself the very opposite of the final victory of grace and life which Jesus announced.

At no point have the most creative and passionate modern religious thinkers been more dialectical than in their quest for the meaning and reality of faith. On the one hand, they have launched a passionate attack upon the typically modern judgment that faith is simply a human phenomenon, a human, all too human projection and fantasy; on the other hand, they have succeeded in pointing to a radically new but uniquely Christian understanding of faith as the human or historical embodiment and actualization of the life and movement of God. We are far from yet reaching a theological appropriation of this achievement, and just as this quest has already followed many paths and been given multiple and diverse expressions, so we may expect a rich variety of new forms of theology.

However, a universal motif of this modern quest for faith is the dialectical principle that the most thorough, most comprehensive, and most total negation either goes hand in hand with or culminates in a correspondingly comprehensive and total affirmation. In one sense, this modern dialectical principle is simply a rebirth and renewal of the classical religious way. For example, we can see its counterpart in Buddhism's absolute negation of the illusion and pain of *samsara* as the hither side of its total affirmation of Nirvana. We can also see its counterpart, and no doubt its historical antecedent, in the biblical expressions of a prophetic and eschatological faith where a

radical condemnation of and opposition to the old form
or aeon of the world is inseparable from a passionate celebration of a new aeon of grace. But modern dialectical
thinkers have given this classical religious way a new
form and expression by abolishing its former limits,
thereby extending faith or dialectical vision throughout
the whole domain of thinking and experience. Thus they
have abolished every distinction between faith and sub-
jectivity, or consciousness and its ground, or the totality
of interior experience and its exterior pole or source.
Only slowly and gradually are we coming today to appre-
ciate the full meaning of this achievement. But it is already clear that the act of negation which is so central in
modern dialectical thinking and vision serves not only to
shatter or dissolve every existing judgment or conception
but also to re-embody these dismembered fragments into
a new and total whole.

Consequently, a truly modern negation of God can by
no means be understood as being a simple or literal negation of God. Nor can it be truly said that a modern negation of God is simply an open or overt expression of a
hidden or interior act of affirmation, as though a false
image or idea of God is negated so as to make possible an
affirmation of the true name of God. What can be truly
said is that a modern negation of God is a total negation
of everything which is manifest and real in consciousness
and experience as God, so as to make possible a radically
new form of consciousness and experience. Thereby a
new form of God appears, but precisely because it is a

radically new form it no longer can be given the name or image of God. Or, more accurately and truly stated, a true negation of God actualizes in a totally new form that which consciousness and faith could once name as God, but which now can be known and named as God only by relapsing or regressing to previous or archaic forms of consciousness and experience. Here lie all the pitfalls and all the illusions of modern expressions of faith, for there is an inevitable tendency to preserve the old God in a new form or image; or, rather, to attempt to perpetuate previous modes of consciousness by dressing them in artificial forms and imagery, adopting the language of empty gesture and hollow speech. It is just for this reason that a genuine dialectical affirmation can be reached only by the most radical negation. Only when all previously existing or presently given forms of consciousness and faith are consistently and totally negated can a new life and consciousness appear and be real. To the extent that previous or given modes of consciousness linger and remain, whether in a conscious or an unconscious form, it is just to that extent that a new language and imagery will be empty and unreal, revealing in its own emptiness the continual presence of the very forms which it claims to have transcended.

Once we reach some understanding of the full movement of dialectical faith and vision, it should become apparent that if full affirmation can be realized only through genuine negation, then the possibility of negation is a necessary ground of affirmation. Then faith can recognize that dying forms of consciousness and society are a consequence of what must be named as grace as well as judgment. For the Christian who lives in expectation of a new aeon of grace, when the Kingdom of God will be all in all, the advent of the possibility of the negation of the deepest ground of faith can be greeted as the way to the realization of faith itself. Thus the appearance to us of an absent and silent God who is humanly unnamable, of a distant and alien God standing wholly beyond consciousness, can be named by faith as the true form and name of God for us. The very emptiness and vacuity of the God who is now manifest to us can make possible faith's negation of God. Through the gift of the passion of Christ the Christian knows that God has given Himself wholly to us, and it is just through this passion that God in Christ is most fully actual in consciousness and experience. So it is that the God who is negated in faith is the God who negated and transcended Himself in Christ, thereby making possible the realization of the new creation which Jesus promised. Certainly the death of God is a Christian symbol, pointing to the center of what the Christian has always known as the passion of Christ. But only in the modern era has the death of God become the center of faith, and in that center we have been given a portal through which to pass to the Christ who is uniquely present and real today, and whom the Christian can know as the revolutionary way to the new life and world ahead of us.

2

The
Kingdom
of God

*

I ✳

It is possible to date the advent of a truly modern form of Christian theology with the historical discovery of the eschatological background and foundation of the New Testament. This discovery was made towards the end of the nineteenth century by Johannes Weiss and Albert Schweitzer, and ever since then it has moved progressively into the center of theological thinking. True, many theological movements have attempted to annul or dissolve or transcend the original historical meaning of an eschatological faith. But that meaning has continued to return and even to enlarge itself despite the efforts to still and negate it. Why has modern theology attempted to negate what has now become all too apparent as the original historical ground and foundation of the Christian faith? This question can be answered quite simply by speaking of the eschatological scandal, the scandal arising from the realization that the proclamation of Jesus and the faith of primitive Christianity are vastly removed historically from all established forms of Christianity.

Before we can understand this scandal we must have some understanding of the original eschatological form of faith. It is now clear that the initial expression of eschatological faith occurred in the reform prophets of the Old Testament. Proclaiming the immediate coming of a new and final time of judgment and salvation, these prophets and their circles appeared to their contemporaries as prophets of doom and destruction, for they envisioned and proclaimed the end of ancient Israel, the final end of the society and religion which was manifest about them. Not only did they violently attack the political, the social, and the economic institutions of their world, and this in the name of the poor, the persecuted, and the oppressed, but they also assaulted the deepest foundations of the faith and religion of ancient Israel. We can see the impact of this assault in their announcement that the day of reward and fulfillment which their people expected would be on the contrary a day of darkness and destruction for Israel. No pre-exilic canonical prophet gave any hope that this destruction could be averted; the most that they promised was the survival of a remnant or the coming of a new and interior covenant to replace the old covenant of Moses. Everything in the message of the reform prophets rested upon the judgment that the old covenant had been violated and thereby annulled. The Lord who had once been known as the source of life and hope for His people was here proclaimed to be the source of a rapidly approaching death and final judgment. Only a radical turning to a new and interior faith in God, a faith arising out of the ashes of the old Israel, could make possible a participation in the new Israel which the prophets promised.

Now we must observe that the new life and salvation proclaimed and envisioned by the reform prophets could become actual only on the basis of the destruction and dissolution of the old Israel. Hence it is a misnomer to call them reform prophets as is commonly done; they were rather revolutionaries, and they called not only for an end to monarchy and feudalism, but also for the destruction and abandonment of Israel's religious forms and traditions. It is well to remember that for these circles the sign of a false prophet is that he predicts a fortunate future for his nation and his people. Here, true faith can be reached only by passing through a full realization of the immediate coming of a total end, and it is this end which we have learned to call eschatological. While the Old Testament prophets did not envision an apocalyptic end of the world, they did envision an end of their own world, a destruction of the human and historical world of ancient Israel. If only for this reason, these prophets were true prophets in a literal sense, for ancient Israel perished in the Exile, and the Judaism and the Torah which evolved as a consequence of the Exile were in large part products of the prophetic movement.

Yet we must give due attention to the fact that the affirmation of a new and eschatological prophetic faith is possible only on the basis of a thoroughgoing negation of the faith and religion which has preceded it. One of the most distinctive marks of the new prophetic faith was that it was so fully dissociated from the social, the political, and the religious institutions of the ancient world. Not only did it negate the mythical and ritual traditions of the ancient Near East, but it set itself against all mythical and cultic forms of religion, thereby dissolving the possibility of social and cultural expressions of faith. The new interior faith for which the prophets called demanded an exodus from all previous forms of religion, and it could establish itself only to the extent that its participants negated all religious relationships to society and the world, thereby freeing themselves from any ultimate dependence upon an historical world which is now known to have been passing away. We might even say that this new prophetic faith transformed an expectation of the immediate coming of a final end into an interior expression of faith, an expression wherein an interior realization of the approaching end of all given forms of consciousness and society brings about a new form of consciousness, and one that by no means can express itself in traditional cultural or religious forms. The radical trust in God for which these prophets called was finally freed from all dependence upon social, political, and religious institutions, and therefore it was a fully individual and interior form of faith.

Unfortunately, it is not possible to trace historically the movement from this prophetic form of eschatological faith to the faith embodied in the New Testament. Doubtless the movements and countermovements leading to this development were very complex, as witness the incorporation of new religious forms from Persia, which later had such an immense impact upon eschatological Judaism. We can, however, see clear lines of continuity, the most important of which for our purpose is the eschatological movement of radical negation. This movement lies at the center of the proclamations of both Jesus and his revolutionary prophetic forebears, and in each case makes possible a radical transition to a new consciousness and life. Just as the Old Testament prophets appeared as no-sayers to their contemporaries, so likewise Jesus pronounced a total judgment upon the human aspirations and values which he met. One difference between Jesus and the earlier prophets is that Jesus never or only incidentally engaged in an open conflict with institutional authority (although, here, as elsewhere, we may simply be the victims of the biases of the Hellenistic editors and writers of the Gospels). Nevertheless, Jesus did attack the human if not the social foundations of all institutional authority, and the radical demands which he placed upon his hearers left no room for obedience to a human authority of any kind. A key image employed by modern New Testament scholarship in its interpretation of the ethical teaching and parables of Jesus is that of reversal, as illustrated by that primal saying of Jesus: "The last will be first, and the first last" (Matthew 20:16). Reversal, in this sense, is found, of course, in Old Testament prophetic oracles, but never therein does it assume the simplicity or the naked power which it commonly has in the words of Jesus.

One means of assessing this sort of difference between Jesus and the prophets is to think of the Old Testament prophets as effecting an initial breakthrough from the society and the religion of the ancient world, with the inevitable result that their language and action bear the impact of their struggles to overcome and transcend that world. Then we may understand that Jesus fully incorporated this breakthrough as the foundation of his own message and ministry, and thus these were freed to engage in an even more comprehensive and total movement of eschatological negation. What is distinctive about this new movement of negation? At this point we must call directly upon modern historical scholarship and recognize that Jesus appeared out of the world of apocalyptic Judaism, the symbolism and imagery of his language as recorded in the Synoptic Gospels is fully apocalyptic, and whatever historical understanding is possible of Jesus can be reached only through apocalyptic or eschatological ideas. Indeed, it is misleading to speak of ideas in this context, for apocalyptic imagery and symbolism have never been given a full theoretical or theological expression. Perhaps the least controversial point which can be made is that apocalyptic faith is the fullest historical expression of an eschatological end.

In apocalyptic faith we find the expectation of the immediate coming of the cosmic end of the world. Whereas the Old Testament prophets announced the coming end of their historical world, or, at most, as in Second Isaiah, envisioned a coming salvation which would bring with it a new form of the cosmos, the fully apocalyptic Judaism out of which Jesus came believed that the cosmic end of the world was immediately at hand. Nor is it possible any longer to think that Jesus did not share this belief. On the contrary, his whole message and ministry can now be seen to be meaningless and unreal apart from it, and it is just this re-alization which constitutes what the Protestant theologian has come to call the eschatological scandal. There are few New Testament scholars today, whether Catholic or Prot-estant, who do not acknowledge this scandal, for the apocalyptic background of the historical Jesus was incon-trovertibly established by the discovery and subsequent investigation of the Dead Sea Scrolls. So when we ask what is distinctive about the movement of eschatological negation in the proclamation of Jesus, we realize that this question can only be answered historically from within the context of apocalyptic Judaism, and this means that the negation lying at the center of Jesus' words and ac-tions is inseparably related to the immediate coming of an absolute transformation of the world.

II ❋

A primary source of confusion in modern interpreta-tions of biblical eschatology derives from the problem posed by the relationship between a messianic hope in the fulfillment of history and an apocalyptic hope in the end of the world. From the time of their entrance into the promised land of Canaan, the ancient Jews lived in hope of a coming day of worldly triumph for both their nation and their God. Throughout the monarchic period of their history, this hope took the form of an expectation of a future sacred king, a king who would be the anointed one (Messiah) of God, and who through God's power would inaugurate a new and final era of justice and peace on earth. In this form there is little that is distinctive about the biblical messianic hope, and we find its counterpart in ancient and even modern monarchies in both the Near and the Far East. True, the messianic hope received its most exalted expression in the prophetic books of the Old Testament, but this very fact has posed one of the most difficult problems of modern Old Testament scholarship. How is it possible that revolutionary prophetic circles who were violently opposed to the institution of the monarchy and even to all worldly power whatsoever could give themselves to the hope in a future sacred monarch? Moreover, there are now good reasons for believing that the messianic prophecies were originally integral components of an enthronement liturgy and served the purpose of announcing a glorious future for a present or an infant king. Is it possible to think that prophetic revolutionaries could so serve the purposes of the institutional authorities whom they so radically opposed?

An even deeper reason for questioning the prophetic identity of the messianic prophecies is that these prophecies so contradict the most fundamental ground of the prophetic oracles themselves. If the nation of Israel faces an immediate destruction, and the most that can be

hoped for in this situation is the survival of a small remnant, then how could such prophets of judgment proclaim the coming triumph of an Israelitic kingdom and its
consequent subjugation of all other nations on earth? Perhaps such inconsistencies are historically possible, but it
seems more likely that when the prophetic writings and
oral traditions were edited, and thence canonized by scri-
bal and priestly authorities, they were assimilated with
priestly and ancient religious forms of belief. In any case
this problem need not unduly trouble the Christian
today, because the messianic hope is consistently attacked and repudiated by Jesus, and its most forceful appearance in the Gospels is in the words of Satan when he
is tempting Jesus to renounce his call and his ministry. It
is true that the title "Messiah" (Christ) is the most universal Christian name of Jesus, but by the time of Jesus the
messianic title of Messiah had become merged in Jewish
eschatological circles with the apocalyptic title of Son of
Man.

The apocalyptic Son of Man is in no sense a future
messianic king; on the contrary, he is a divine and celestial judge and redeemer who in the last days will appear
in the heavens with legions of angels to inaugurate the
Kingdom of God. The distance between the pure forms of
the messianic and the apocalyptic hopes can be measured
by the distance lying between a messianic expectation of
the coming of a new historical era on earth and an apocalyptic expectation of the coming of a new aeon or new
creation or new world. The one lives in hope of the trans-

formation of history, making possible the advent of a new man and new society; but the other lives in hope of the transformation of the cosmos, of all reality whatsoever, therein making possible not a new society or a new man but rather a new being or new creation. Messianic hopes, despite their utopianism, are resolutely this-worldly; they seek a new justice and a new righteousness in our world. But apocalyptic hopes are manifestly other-worldly; they look forward to the destruction or dissolution of this world as an indispensable prelude to the birth of a new world. Indeed, apocalyptic faith shares a common religious ground with its counterpart in Oriental mysticism, for both seek a total dissolution or reversal of everything which is manifest and real as world. For only such a total reversal or end of the world can make possible the advent of what the apocalyptic believer envisions as the Kingdom of God.

We must not confuse the apocalyptic symbol of the Kingdom of God with the Old Testament symbol of the Kingship of God. The latter envisions God as the true Lord of His chosen people, from whom alone all authority and power ultimately derives, and who is moreover the sole Governor of all history. While the Old Testament symbol of the Kingship of God envisions God as the one absolutely sovereign Monarch and Lord, the apocalyptic symbol of the Kingdom of God envisions that Kingdom as the absolute antithesis of all worldly power and authority, and therefore the Kingdom of God can only appear and be real with the passing away and final end of the world.

Now there can no longer be any question that the symbolic center of Jesus' proclamation is the apocalyptic symbol of the Kingdom of God. Not only does he begin his ministry with the announcement that the Kingdom of God is dawning or at hand but the great majority of his words and actions can be shown to be grounded in an apocalyptic expectation. If only for this reason, the Jesus who is portrayed in the Gospels is not truly tempted by social or political revolution, nor is he concerned with institutional reform of any kind; for with the final realization of the Kingdom of God all these things will pass away.

Once again we must compare and contrast Jesus with his prophetic predecessors. While it is possible to say that the Old Testament prophets were apolitical and had no interest in political and social institutions as such, they were leaders of the opposition against the monarchy, and they hurled violent curses at all who are attached to social power or economic prosperity. Nothing is more evident in the prophetic oracles than an opposition to all forms of worldly power. Such power is identified by the prophets as a primary cause of Israel's having turned away from the Lord; hence they issued calls for repentance which demanded a repudiation and negation of all worldly power, for only a turning away from the power of the world can now make possible a turning to faith and trust in God. Jesus also attacked the rich and the powerful and exalted the poor and the weak, but he did so in the context of an eschatological situation which was here understood to be ushering in a total reversal of all worldly conditions. The prophets expected a judgment which would destroy Israel as a worldly nation and society; hence they called for a repentance from their hearers which would both relieve them of the guilt deriving from a participation in a corrupt power and prepare them for the loss of all such power. Unlike the prophets, Jesus expected the immediate coming of the end of the world; accordingly, his sayings seldom if ever focus upon political or social problems as such, and he in no way prepares his hearers for a new historical situation. Therefore Jesus was even more utopian than the prophets, and his demands have no contact at all with the pragmatic world of social and political action.

Max Weber, who was the first scholar to reach a critical understanding of the social and political significance of the ancient prophets, strongly emphasizes that the prophets never raised the question of the mythical or cosmic meaning of the world. Just as the ecstasy of the Old Testament prophet did not lead to deification, nor emancipate the prophet from an unreal or sinful world, so likewise the prophetic experience entailed no special interpretation of the world. All the energy of the prophet is directed to a radical demand for moral action and faithful witness rather than to a quest for metaphysical or cosmological understanding. This is due to what Weber terms the "psychic economy" of the prophets, which channels all the prophets' energy into a new ethical obedience to the Lord, a radical obedience occasioned by the immi-

nence of a final judgment. We can see a significant parallel
to this prophetic indifference to the mythical or cosmological meaning of the world in the Buddha's repudiation
of all metaphysical questioning, and in both cases this
questioning is negated or set aside to make possible a
total participation in a concrete way to salvation or release.

At this point we may also observe an important difference between the proclamation of Jesus and the apocalyptic religion of many of his contemporaries. Jewish apocalypticism, as witness the Qumran sects who produced
the Dead Sea Scrolls, was much given to the pursuit of
esoteric knowledge, to speculations and visions of the
exact course of those final historical and cosmic events
which would culminate in the end of time. But Jesus insisted that no man could know the exact time of the last
day or hour, and he clearly subordinated or eliminated all
cosmic and historical visions in his proclamation and para-
bolic enactment of the dawning of the Kingdom of God.
There is nothing comparable to the Sermon on the Mount
in Jewish apocalyptic literature, or, for that matter, in the
New Testament book of Revelation, and this might lead us
to surmise that the faith and obedience which Jesus demanded left no room for cosmological or even historical understanding. Jesus left us no prophecies of coming political
events, no visions of future social chaos and destruction,
and no prophecies directed to particular individuals and
social groups. All these affairs of the world are completely
irrelevant, for the total end is immediately at hand. In Jesus

we are confronted with the purely apocalyptic and eschatological prophet, the prophet who gives no attention to any
merely human or worldly problem, and who embodies in
his words and actions an absolute negation and transcendence of everything which is immediately or apparently
manifest as humanity and world. Only in the Buddha can
we find an historical figure who is truly comparable to
Jesus.

III ✳

Once one has been given an eschatological key to the
New Testament, then the great body of the New Testament writings, including the epistles of Paul, assumes a
new pattern and meaning, and it does so with such power
as to place in question every previous method of New
Testament interpretation. While it is true that ever since
the establishment of the canon of the New Testament a
wide variety of sectarian bodies have grounded themselves
in an eschatological form of faith, these bodies have always
been repudiated or expelled by the dominant forms of
Christianity, and with such success that the modern historical demonstration of the eschatological foundation of the
New Testament appeared to Christian scholarly and theological circles as a revolutionary discovery. It cannot be accidental that this "discovery" occurred at a time when
Christendom was in a virtual state of collapse, its roots having withered away, and thus the established historical
forms of Christianity no longer had the power to bind their

adherents to traditional or orthodox patterns of belief. As Kierkegaard had prophetically foreseen, the Christianity of the New Testament no longer exists, and the whole historical evolution of Christianity has been of such a kind as to make its modern form exactly the opposite of what it is in the New Testament.

At no point has this peculiarly modern scandal of faith been more powerful than in the challenge which it has brought to the Christian doctrine of God. If, as now seems clear, Christianity evolved historically by way of abolishing and dissolving its original eschatological foundation, then the God who is the ground of the established forms of Christianity will of necessity be alienated and estranged from the Kingdom of God which Jesus proclaimed. This is clearly the case, for there now appears to be no way whatsoever of establishing a positive theological correlation between the Christian doctrine of God and the original Christian symbol of the Kingdom of God. Indeed, a contemporary theological inquiry into the meaning of Kingdom of God must begin by confessing that theology as such has lost nearly all sense of the original meaning of this primary Christian symbol. The God who has been the ground and goal of the Christian theological quest is the God who alone is God, the transcendent God who exists eternally and autonomously as the sole cause of Himself, and whose very Being creates a chasm between Himself and the world. Not only has God been traditionally conceived as inactive, impassive, and unmoving, but His transcendent Lordship has been conceived in such a manner as to make it inconceivable that He Himself or His own Being could be present or active at the center of the movement and actuality of the world.

Christians have commonly conceived of the Kingdom of God as the rule or the reign or the Lordship of God, thus perpetuating the root theological idea that God can be immanently present in the world only in the form of His transcendent identity. There can be no possibility here of understanding God as an active, a mobile, or a forward-moving God, except insofar as He is understood to act in such a manner as to reveal His original power and glory. Nor can the Kingdom of God be understood by this means as an eschatological culmination or realization of the forward movement of God Himself. On the contrary, exactly the opposite is true, for to conceive the Kingdom of God as the reign or the Lordship of God is to identify the Kingdom of God with God's original or primordial relationship to the world. Inevitably, Christian images of the reign and the Lordship of God are images of the primordial power of God. They are symbolic statements about the original relationship between an absolutely sovereign Creator and His totally dependent or contingent creation. Therefore to conceive God's Kingdom as His primordial power is to understand God's ultimate or final relation to the world as being identical with the original or prefallen relationship of the world to God. Then the world is manifest quite simply as the creation; it embodies no movement or turn away from God, but rather exists in an integral and harmonious relationship with its Creator.

By this path Christianity has understood Jesus' eschatological proclamation as a call to the world or to a fallen humanity to return to its original or primordial relationship to God. Ironically, the final or eschatological act of God which Jesus envisioned and proclaimed here becomes wholly reversed; it becomes exactly the opposite of its original meaning. The God of the End now appears wholly in the form and visage of the God of the Beginning; the Creator God is now the God of final judgment and salvation. A faith which was originally directed to a future and final end now becomes directed to the intrinsic opposite of that end, the initial or primordial state of the creation. Omega becomes alpha, the last days of the world are transposed into the first days of the creation, and the end of the world is transposed into the dawn of the creation. Above all, Jesus' eschatological pointing to the End becomes transformed into a backward call to return to the lost innocence of the primordial Beginning. Is it any wonder that Christianity has evolved to the opposite of its original identity? Or is it at all remarkable that the modern discovery of the eschatological identity of the historical Jesus should have come as a revolutionary and cataclysmic shock to the Christian world?

We must further note that Christians have come to believe that they share a common conception of God with Muslims and Jews. Or, at least, most Christians and most theologians believe that the God whom the Christian calls Father is the same God whom Israel knows as Yahweh and Islam as Allah. In other words, the Christian commonly has no qualms about confessing that the God whom he knows as God can truly be known as God apart from Jesus Christ. Here, Jesus' proclamation of the final triumph of the Kingdom of God need have no effect upon the believer's understanding of the nature and identity of God Himself. Or, rather, when Jesus' work and message are understood as leading or pointing a fallen world to its pristine and unfallen state, then the God of the End can truly be known as the God of the Beginning, and all men can be understood as worshiping a common God. Thereby Jesus becomes a new Moses, faith is conceived as being eternally and universally the same, and the new covenant or new testament becomes quite simply a renewal or repetition of the old. Christianity can then be presented as the universal and absolute religion, as that religion which most fully understands and submits to God the Creator, and therefore as that religion which can most effectively bring about a return of a fallen humanity to its original communion with God. So likewise all religions can here be understood as being preparations for Christianity: for all religions bear the impact of the original Fall, and insofar as they attempt to reverse the Fall they prepare their followers for that absolute reversal of the Fall which has occurred in the uniquely Christian Christ.

It is precisely when Jesus is understood as embodying

in his work and words an absolute reversal of the Fall that he can be most fully accepted by the established forms of Christianity as revealing the true identity of God. Only when the effects of the original Fall have been wholly annulled and erased can humanity return to the pristine glance of Adam and behold the true nature of God. Then God's sovereign power can appear as gracious power, His Lordship as fatherhood, and His judgment as acceptance. Then the transcendence of God will be manifest as the immanence of God, the awesome and distant God will be one with the near and the sustaining God, and God will be fully real to faith as God. The cry of the Christian then becomes, Let God be truly God and the world be truly the creation, both existing in their original relation to each other. God's final or eschatological act can then be understood as the full epiphany or reappearance of God's original or primordial relationship to the world. The eschatological events of salvation can then be known as the final renewal of the Creator's original Lordship over the creation. And the finality of Christ can then be apprehended as the full appearance in Jesus Christ of the original glory and power of God.

These are consequences of the Christian choice to allow God to be fully God. But if we are now forced to make the judgment that the historical movement and evolution of Christianity has negated and reversed its original eschatological ground, then to recover and renew that ground we must negate and reverse the Christian affirmation of God. Moreover, it is precisely by reversing the established Christian doctrine of God as the Creator that we can become open to an eschatological conception of the identity and movement of God. Only when the Kingdom of God is understood as the intrinsic opposite of the original relationship of God to the world can the Kingdom of God be grasped as a truly new and future reality. To the extent that faith is bound to the primordial identity and nature of God, it must be closed to the eschatological movement of God. So it is that a faith which chose to give itself totally to the primordial God not only reversed the eschatological proclamation of Jesus but totally closed itself to the eschatological meaning of God and the world. Just as the forward movement of eschatological faith was reversed by the backward movement of a priestly and ecclesiastical Christianity, so a radical and eschatological Christianity must reverse the established meaning and identity of God. There is no other way to an eschatological faith today, for it is Christian faith in God and a consequent Christian doctrine of God which has most deeply annulled and reversed the original eschatological ground of faith.

IV ✳

If there is one assured or almost certain result of New Testament scholarship regarding the original proclamation of Jesus, it is the thesis that Jesus proclaimed a Kingdom of God which is dawning in the world, even if it could not be known to the man of unbelief. Dawning is a

crucial image unveiling Jesus' vision of the final or eschatological time. For the Kingdom of God which Jesus proclaimed is both present and future; it has not yet arrived
in its final form, but nevertheless is already working in
advance, and is even now present as an inbreaking realm
of final salvation. Therefore Jesus proclaimed the advent
of an eschatological event of absolutely decisive significance. The gospel or "good news" which he joyously announced could only have derived from an apprehension
of an eschatological or final act of God Himself. There
can be no possibility here of thinking of the eschatological time as a consequence of a reborn or renewed faith in
God, as though the renewal and intensification of an ancient faith in God could usher in a whole new situation of
the world in relation to God. The Kingdom of God to
which Jesus points is a Kingdom which actualizes or realizes itself; it is in no sense the product of a merely human
act, and therefore it must be understood as the realization
of an act or movement of God.

Before we can become open to an eschatological conception of God, we must reach an understanding of a
God who is capable of a final and definitive act, an act
making God present and real in the world in a wholly
new manner and mode. Such an act can usher in a whole
new reality of salvation only by transforming the original
or primordial relation between God and the world. To
speak in this sense of the Kingdom of God is to speak of a
new and final form or manifestation of God. Not in the
sense that God's eternal glory and sovereignty is now be-

coming manifest to the world, but rather in the sense that the actualization of the Kingdom of God realizes a new and final mode of God's own existence and Being. If the Kingdom of God is dawning here and now, then God Himself is actually breaking into the world, and therefore He must be present and manifest in a new form. Of course, the eschatological presence and manifestation of God bring with it a total and cataclysmic transformation of the world. A fully eschatological faith, as Paul says, knows that the form or schema of this world is passing away, and passing away precisely because of the advent or dawning of God's Kingdom. Thus the world itself can no longer appear to faith in its original form, except insofar as it is known as old aeon or old creation. Yet if the dawning of the Kingdom of God effects such a radical transformation of faith's apprehension of the world, should we not expect an equally radical transformation of faith's apprehension of God?

Why is it that the Christian even today is so reluctant to think of Jesus' proclamation as speaking of an act or movement of God Himself? Is it because we know that Jesus' proclamation is fully eschatological and we cannot conceive the theological possibility of a final or ultimate act of God? But are we not thereby bound once again to the "mystery" of religion, a mystery which Jesus promised to bring to an end, by our very refusal to entertain the possibility that Jesus was speaking in a new and radical way of the innermost reality of God? Can the Christian really believe that the deepest offense of Jesus' message and ministry was that he sought out the outcast and the impious, and not that he was truly speaking blasphemously about God? Is it true that the offense of Jesus' proclamation is identical with the offense induced by the ancient prophets and that no new prophet arose in Israel in him? Indeed, is it possible for the Christian to believe, as many New Testament scholars and theologians have come to affirm, that there is no new word or revelation in Jesus? No, if the Christian is to respond to Jesus with total seriousness he must look upon him as the revealer who unveiled the final mystery of God.

At this point dualism must be avoided at all costs. The Kingdom of God is not the manifestation of a new or strange God. On the contrary, it is the final manifestation of the God who has previously revealed Himself in history; or, at least, in that history which reaches a consummation in this moment of its ultimate expression. Nevertheless, the God who undergoes a final movement or realization of Himself cannot realize or actualize that movement apart from a negation and transcendence of His previous manifestations. We are not to imagine that an eschatological act of God is a consummation of a continuous process of enlarging and enriching the primordial nature of God. For to think in this manner is to close the possibility of an eschatological or apocalyptic end, an end which is truly the end, so truly the end that nothing whatsoever is unaffected by its actualization. Everything which precedes that end must be affected by its realization, and so affected as to bring to an end its previous form and identity. This does not mean that we must think of an eschatological end as a literal end, as though everything quite simply perished in its realization. But it does mean that everything is transformed in the realization of a final end, not in the sense that it is merely given a new form and appearance, but rather that it here achieves a new reality and identity. No longer can the new be truly named by the old names and images. Or, if the ancient names must perforce be employed, an eschatological situation demands that the new be evoked only by way of reversing all given and established meaning. Ancient names and images will then embody the opposite of their original meaning: new aeon, new creation, new humanity, and, above all, Kingdom of God!

The intention of apocalyptic language is not simply to negate but also to invert and reverse all given and established meaning. The new creation is by no means to be understood simply as a new form of the old; it is far rather to be understood as the opposite of the old, and it can only be named or evoked at a time when the old creation appears as old or dying. Yet it is one creation, one world, which is named apocalyptically by the opposing images of old and new. All too clearly apocalyptic faith lives in expectation of the immediate coming of the end of the old creation; yet out of the destruction or dissolution of the old creation will appear and be born the new creation, the Kingdom of God. Literalism would have it that a physical heaven or kingdom will appear as a result of the literal destruction of the world; but this is not only manifestly absurd, it also violates a fundamental intention of apocalyptic language. True apocalyptic language, to judge by the standard of Jesus' eschatological proclamation, envisions or evokes a new reality which reverses the form and actuality of a given reality. This pattern of reversal is found, of course, in the ancient prophetic oracles, but in its full apocalyptic form it so succeeds in reversing all given meaning as to give to the whole of reality a new form and face. It is not that the old creation must literally cease to be if the new creation is to be real, but rather that everything which is manifest and actual as world must perish if a truly and fully new actuality of the world is to be realized.

At the very least, true apocalyptic symbols and images must point to or embody a total reversal of all meaning, of all value, of all actuality, and of all identity. Apocalyptic language pierces to the center of that which is immediately apparent and real, inverting that center so as to reverse the meaning of a given world, thereby making possible the celebration of the presence and activity of an opposite world. Thus apocalyptic images are opposite images—old and new, light and darkness, flesh and Spirit —but they are not opposite in a dualistic sense. To evoke apocalyptically the presence of the new is to shatter and reverse the presence and manifestation of the old. Not until the appearance and manifestation of a given and established reality is wholly reversed can that reality achieve its own apocalyptic resolution. Here, every given identity must pass into its own intrinsic opposite, must become its own inherent other, if an apocalyptic reversal is to occur. Such a reversal is not a literal negation of the reality which it affects, it is rather a total transformation of the meaning and actuality of that reality, thereby allowing it to evolve into a wholly new form and identity.

Is it possible to speak of an apocalyptic reversal of God Himself? Can we understand an eschatological act of God to be a final realization in a new form and identity of the primordial God? Can a final actualization of the life and movement of God be understood to occur by way of the negation and transcendence of the primordial form and identity of God? Can the new immanence of the Kingdom of God be apprehended as the intrinsic opposite or inherent other of the original transcendence of God? These are the questions which will establish the possibility or impossibility of an eschatological conception of God. But first we must attempt to speak in a new way of the transcendence and immanence of God. Is it possible to understand pure transcendence as a symbolic image of the primordial God and pure immanence as a symbolic image of the Kingdom of God? That is to say, can we think of radical transcendence as a true image of the original identity of God, and of radical immanence as a true image of the final identity of God? In this sense, can immanence and transcendence be understood as the inherent and integral opposites of each other? If so, is it possible to conceive the possibility of an eschatological movement from transcendence to immanence, a total

movement whereby the fullness of transcendence passes
into a final immanence?

V ✳

The fundamental problem at hand is the question of
whether the Christian God can truly be known as a process or movement which actualizes and realizes itself by
way of passing into the opposite of its own original identity. Rather than conceive God as an unchanging and immobile Being, is it possible in faith to conceive God as an
evolving and forward-moving process, a total process
carrying forward the fullness of its own life and movement into new forms and identities? Can we entertain the
possibility that God's own life and energy evolves by way
of a continuous and total eschatological movement, a
movement from a primordial beginning to an eschatological end? Can we conceive faith itself and its own historical evolution as either a positive or a negative response to
and embodiment of the life and movement of God? Thus
if the dominant historical movement of Christianity has
been one wherein it has moved ever more fully and finally into an understanding and apprehension of God as
the primordial Creator, as the absolutely sovereign and
transcendent Lord, is it possible to reverse that movement and seek to apprehend and understand God fully
and finally as the totally immanent and actualized Kingdom of God? Is such a reversal already present in the

proclamation of Jesus and in the eschatological faith of primitive Christianity as well as in those apocalyptic movements which have ever challenged the dominant and established forms of Christianity?

Such an approach may well give us not only a new mode of entry into the proclamation of Jesus but also a genuinely eschatological understanding of the movement and identity of the Christian God. We can realize by this means that the transcendence and immanence of God are neither eternal attributes of God nor unchanging or eternally given forms and manifestations of God. They are rather continually evolving but yet mutually opposing expressions of the life and movement of God. Immanence is the inherent or integral opposite of transcendence, just as transcendence is of immanence, and only in relation to its own inherent other can either most truly and actually be itself. Accordingly, neither transcendence nor immanence can here be conceived as fixed or given, either in terms of its own intrinsic identity, or in terms of its relation to the other. Each evolves and is real in relation to the other, and the movement of each must either still or reverse the direction and form of the other. Thus the full appearance and actualization of the transcendence of God must dissolve and negate the immanence of God, just as the final realization and embodiment of the immanence of God must annul and reverse the transcendence of God.

Once again we are faced with the temptation of dualism, the temptation of thinking of transcendence and immanence as simple opposites, as though each were only the opposite of the other. Perhaps we can meet this challenge by returning to the perspective of the original and fundamental eschatological ground of the Christian faith, attempting to relate that ground to our understanding of immanence and transcendence. Is it possible to understand transcendence not only as the primary symbol of the primordial nature and identity of God but also as the symbolic point from which the eschatological movement of God originates? That is to say, can we understand transcendence as the fundamental and original ground of an eschatological movement? By this means we could understand transcendence as an essential and necessary ground of an eschatological movement, a ground apart from whose presence and reality no eschatological movement could occur and be real. Thereby we could also realize that pure transcendence is the original form and identity of an eschatological process which finally will culminate in pure immanence. Accordingly, the eschatological movement of God would occur by way of a continual passage or transition *from* transcendence *to* immanence.

This eschatological process, however, should not be thought of as occurring immediately or at once. Nor should it be understood as moving continually and progressively in the same direction and form, as though it were always manifest and actual as a movement from beginning to end. For a theological conception of the eschatological movement of God must take account of the complexity, the richness, the variety, and the seeming contradictions of the epiphanies or manifestations of God in the biblical and Christian traditions. There can be no possibility here of conceiving a movement of God which moves openly and clearly from an original to a final expression. It should far rather be conceived as a comprehensive process embodying the realization of its life and energy through a long and complex series of movements and countermovements between its respective poles. Then only the actual expression of these movements and countermovements would free or release the divine life and energy for a real movement from a beginning to an end. What is vitally important for a theological understanding of the eschatological identity of God is that such a real movement be grasped as being not only possible but necessary. Otherwise, all movements of the divine process must finally be judged to be illusory or unreal, or real only insofar as they reflect the history of the consciousness of faith, and thus real only inasmuch as they are a human phenomenon. But to follow this path is to deny and refuse a fully eschatological faith, and thus to renounce the fundamental ground of Christianity.

Let us recall the crucial movement of the early Christian form of eschatological faith: a movement from old to new in the context of the imminent collapse of the old. Not only does a new aeon here dawn in faith itself in such a manner as to shatter the old, but faith in this form is possible only by virtue of a new and radical freedom from the totality of old aeon or old creation, including its religion and its God. Only on the basis of an interior participation in both the dawning of a new time and world and the dissolution or disintegration of the old time and world can an apocalyptic faith in its full form become actualized and real. Indeed, the believer participates in and himself embodies the new aeon only to the extent that he has been liberated from and has thus transcended the old aeon. He can be open to the new only insofar as he has been freed from the old. Allowing this model to stand forth as a witness to the eschatological movement of God, we could then understand God as reaching or realizing the fullness and finality of His own immanence only by way of negating and reversing His own transcendent ground. Such a negation would be a real negation, a real and actual movement, and yet its very movement of negating transcendence is precisely the occasion for the embodiment and realization of a pure and final immanence. Can we not by this means come to understand that it is the passage or transition of transcendence into immanence which is the ground of the eschatological movement of God?

Hence by this route we can see that there is not simply a divine movement from transcendence to immanence but that transcendence realizes or fulfills itself by passing into immanence. Immanence is opposed to transcendence in the sense that immanence *is* that which transcendence *was*. We could also say that only insofar as the primordial ground of the divine process is itself transcended can that ground realize its own intrinsic or final resolution. Thus, from this point of view, the divine process is a dual process: its negation of its own original and transcendent ground is also and simultaneously an actualization and realization of its immanent and final identity. But this is a dual process in a crucial sense, for neither movement can be real apart from the other, and neither can occur apart from the other. Properly stated, we should have to say that each movement is the reverse side of the other, so that the negation of transcendence does not simply make possible the realization of immanence; it is itself that realization, for here negation and affirmation are ultimately one. Nevertheless, it is of vital importance from the perspective of the Christian faith to understand this dual and dialectical movement as a forward-moving process. Only thereby will it be possible to understand the Kingdom of God as the immanent actualization and realization of the primordial and transcendent Creator.

Is there a real possibility of conjoining or uniting the symbolic names of Creator and Kingdom of God? There certainly is; for have we not already observed that Christianity has finally identified the Kingdom of God with the primordial majesty of the Creator? Insofar as we have also noted that this identification can be reached only by reversing the eschatological movement of biblical faith, we have only to point to a negation and reversal of the Christian understanding of God in order to perceive the path to an understanding of the Kingdom of God as the eschatological embodiment of the Creator. Yet no true way lies to this goal apart from a comprehensive and thoroughgoing transformation of the whole body of the dominant historical expressions of Christian belief. Thus the goal lies far before us, so far as to make its realization seem all but unthinkable. Nonetheless, if we can but grasp the pattern and form of an eschatological movement, realizing ourselves that it can realize and actualize its future only by negating and reversing its past, then we shall be prepared to see that it is only an ultimate and total act of negation which can embody and make real a truly eschatological consummation. And even though that negation may ultimately be known as affirmation, humanly it can appear only as negation, and as an ultimate negation and final death, as the death of God Himself.

3

The
Descent
Into
Hell

*

I ✳

Yet another path into an understanding of a divine and eschatological movement of total negation is by way of conceiving a negation of that given meaning of God which lies most deeply buried within ourselves. When we inquire into this given meaning of God, whether by means of interior introspection or by an investigation of those images of God which have most deeply affected our history and our consciousness, we are confronted by the fundamental idea of the impassable mystery and unknowability of God. The name of God most immediately appears to us as the name of an ultimate mystery, a mystery which can be unveiled by no human act of naming, and which cannot be truly penetrated by any human form of knowledge or vision. God is the unsayable, the unknowable, the unnamable: or, His is a name which can only truly be spoken by Himself, by His own act of revelation. Then the God who speaks or reveals Himself is the God who speaks out of the heart of

97

darkness, out of an impenetrable mystery, a mystery which can be uncovered by no act or movement of man. Indeed, the presence of God can only be a mysterious presence, an awesome and eternally elusive presence, a presence which unfolds itself only to the extent that its own mystery is embodied in the eye of its beholder.

Now we must not simply recognize the living power of this ancient image of God; we must also realize, as our century has done, that an image of the total mystery of God has become more deeply embedded in our time than ever hitherto in history, and is pervasively present not only in our faith and theological understanding but also in our critical thinking and our imaginative vision. Long gone are those periods in our history when it was possible to have an innate sense of the actual identity of God, or a moral assurance as to the purpose or providence of God. No longer is the name of God evoked at the center of life and understanding; it is now spoken only at the peripheries, in those boundary situations where understanding and experience break down. God has increasingly and ever more comprehensively become for us a name of total and ultimate mystery, a mystery in the presence of which we can neither act nor speak. One has only to examine the most powerful works of modern literature, even those written by seemingly Christian writers, to recognize that the name of God can never truly be spoken by us in moments of joy or affirmation. It is rather on those occasions which numb or dissolve the possibility of speech that the name of God is most forcefully evoked. And then it evokes the nameless which can never truly be named or envisioned, that inaudible and formless power which evokes itself on our lips with the name of God.

The mystery which we evoke and even embody in ourselves when we speak the name of God is a mystery associated with an infinitely distance beyond. Whether this beyond appears to us as lying within the mysterious depths of our unconscious or as lying outside the boundary of everything which we can know as time and space, it is manifest as an alien beyond, a beyond standing over and against man and the world. If we no longer can shudder with dread in the presence of such an alien beyond, we know an empty and pervasive numbness which is its surrogate, a blank hollowness instilling us with the dehumanizing consequences of contact with a totally alien power. Only in ancient Gnostic imagery of an alien God and an alien cosmos can we discover a full historical parallel to the imagery of the beyond which has come to dominate the modern imagination. Moreover, both in Gnosticism and in modern imagery the alien beyond is manifest as being both within and without, both interior and exterior, as its alien otherness appears as the ground of both individual identity and universal life. We may envision the beyond as lying in either the heights or the depths; but in either case we know it as an alien beyond, so alien that humanly it is impossible to speak or envision it. Need we marvel that many Protestant theologians can now rejoice that the gospel frees us from all images of God!

Without even attempting to cast a glance at the long and complex history lying behind this contemporary image of total otherness, it is immediately apparent that no such image is present in what we have come to know and understand as the words and actions of Jesus. So far from being a distant and alien other, the beyond which Jesus proclaims and symbolically enacts is the opposite of a beyond which is manifest as the wholly other. Jesus points neither to the heights nor to the depths, neither to an infinitely distant beyond nor to an infinitely hidden within, but rather to that beyond, and that beyond alone, which breaks into world and existence here and now. Humanly considered, perhaps nothing so clearly distinguishes the modern and the primitive Christian as the joy with which the early Christian heard and proclaimed the gospel. For how could the modern Christian rejoice in the presence of what he has come to know as God? At most he can find peace in the stilling or the veiling of the name and the image of God. Yet the beyond which appears in Jesus, or which is manifest in his words and acts, is a beyond whose presence or realization makes possible for those who know it an immediate and ecstatic joy.

It is not uncommon for critical interpreters of the New Testament, particularly when they are discussing the parables of Jesus, to speak of the mystery of the Kingdom of God. Certainly a mystery is present in these parables, just as it is in all those words and actions with which Jesus unveils the dawning of the Kingdom. But it is imperative that we compare this mystery with the mystery which we

have come to associate with the name of God. Once again
the image of reversal provides us with a key to the meaning of an eschatological proclamation. For the Kingdom
of God which Jesus proclaims reverses all those hopes
and expectations with which his contemporaries sought
its advent. On the one hand, the Kingdom to which he
points is not a kingdom of this world, not a messianic or
human kingdom. On the other hand, it is not a kingdom
of another world, not a celestial or a heavenly kingdom
which appears only beyond and apart. On the contrary,
the Kingdom of God which Jesus proclaims is a distant
and transcendent beyond which dawns here and now: in
this world, in this time, and in this place. The mystery of
the Kingdom does not truly reside in its apparent transcendent otherness, but rather in its actual advent: for the
dawning of the Kingdom shatters and reverses all previous images of God. Most deeply of all, it shatters the
images of the transcendence and the mystery of God, and
not only shatters but reverses them: for here the mystery
of God comes to bear the opposite of its original and
given meaning.

We can apprehend something of the significance of this
reversal by noting that here the Kingdom is neither an
awesome and majestic otherness nor a sovereign and
overwhelming power. True, the disciples of Jesus associated the advent of the Kingdom with innumerable miracles, and all too traditional miracles at that. But Jesus
repudiated the quest for miracles, and radically dissociated the faith for which he called from a miraculous or

otherworldly base. We must also take due note of the fact that Jesus directed his ministry away from the pious and the religious, away from those who had an assurance of the presence and sustenance of the living and transcendent Lord. We have long since learned that in attacking the Pharisees Jesus was not attacking the hypocritical in any obvious or manifest sense—for we know or should know that the Pharisees were the most deeply religious leaders of his day; Jesus was rather engaged in an assault upon the fundamental forms of an established and given faith in God. Moreover, it is just this faith in God which most decisively turns the believer away from the dawning of the Kingdom. Hence Jesus not only sought out the outcast and the impious; he also fulfilled his own calling in such a manner as not only to shock but to outrage the "religious," and the religious in this sense could only be those who were most confident of their faith in God.

Is it not all too obvious that the more powerful the faith of a believer in a distant and transcendent God, the more he will be turned away from or hardened against a Kingdom of God which is dawning here and now? It is not moral hypocrisy or an empty faith which is the deepest obstacle to an acceptance of the advent of the Kingdom; it is rather a deep and living faith in the transcendent and primordial Creator, a faith which is a response to the transcendent form and identity of God. The believer who is bound to faith in the purely transcendent God is bound to a mystery lying wholly beyond and apart, a mystery which cannot be unveiled by an act or movement of man, but only by an act or revelation of God coming to man from without. Such a believer will look "above" or "beyond" for the advent of the Kingdom, or will prepare himself for its coming by immersing himself in the revealed, and hence previously established, images of God. Thereby he will be totally unprepared for a Kingdom dawning at the center of life and the world, a transcendence realizing itself here and now in the initial expressions of its new and total immanence. As the parables of Jesus make abundantly clear, it is our naming of God, our turning away to the majestic and transcendent God, which veils and hides the working of the Kingdom. The "mystery" of the Kingdom derives from the mystery of God; or, rather, the mystery which we impute to the Kingdom derives from our bondage to the ancient mystery and transcendence of God.

In one sense it is surely possible to say that the work of Jesus was the task of inverting and reversing all those given images of God which lay both before and about him. There was nothing new in this calling as such, it was exercised by the prophets before him, and if anything it was exercised far more violently by earlier prophets than by Jesus. If we were to distinguish Jesus from the prophets at this point it could only be by way of establishing the more radical act of inversion present in Jesus' eschatological proclamation—an inversion shattering the most fundamental ground of all previous images of God. Once all witness to God is comprehended in an eschatological pointing to the dawning of the Kingdom of God, then that transcendent form of God which is apprehended as standing aloof and apart from this dawning itself becomes the object of a prophetic and eschatological assault. Indeed, it is precisely the aloofness and apartness of the transcendent God, the infinite distance and awesome majesty of God, which is negated by the eschatological actualization and realization of God. Hence a bondage to the God who is infinitely beyond becomes the deepest obstacle to an acceptance of the advent of the Kingdom of God. Only a dissolution of the mystery of God makes possible a manifestation of the Kingdom of God. In Jesus we encounter the eschatological prophet who effects an absolute reversal of that mystery: "Behold, the kingdom of God is in your midst" (Luke 17:21).

II ❋

When we pass from the historical Jesus to the faith and community which embodied his work and proclamation, we may observe a revolutionary turning or transformation. Critical study has now all but established the crucial point that Jesus did not point to himself in his eschatological proclamation, not even to himself as the promised Son of Man. Everything in Jesus' words and actions points to the advent or dawning of the Kingdom, a dawning so all-encompassing as to negate and dissolve every other center of attention or apprehension. But, in the faith of the early church, the original bearer of the eschatological proclamation was drawn into the proclamation itself and became its essential content. We are indebted to Rudolf Bultmann and his school for the full establishment of this vitally important historical insight, an insight most incisively expressed in those seminal words of Bultmann: "The proclaimer became the proclaimed." Not only did the eschatological proclaimer become the eschatological Saviour, but with the birth of Hellenistic Christianity Jesus became cultically worshiped as *Kyrios* or Lord. In no sense may we look upon this historical movement as an evolutionary or organic development in Newman's sense, for it neither preserves its original ground nor is it in continuity with its original form. On the contrary, this was precisely the path by which Christianity reversed and negated its eschatological ground, and gradually but ever more comprehensively evolved into the opposite of its original faith and vision.

Let us once again take up a primal or given religious meaning and identity, this time directing our attention to the given meaning of Jesus or the Christ in the established and dominant forms of Christianity. Already in the New Testament, and most emphatically in the letters of Paul, Christ is apprehended as *Christus Victor*, as the triumphant and resurrected Lord. The Jesus of faith is the resurrected Jesus, the Jesus who has triumphed over the passion and the crucifixion by his resurrection and ascension into heaven. What most demands attention here is not the simple or literal event of resurrection but rather the form and meaning which the resurrection assumes in the apprehension of faith. Granted that there are a number of images of the resurrection in the New Testament and in early Christian literature, what most stands out in these images in terms of their relation to the proclamation of Jesus? Can we not see quite clearly that they reverse the direction and goal of the dawning Kingdom? Whereas the Kingdom is a dawning here and now of a transcendent beyond, the resurrected Christ became for Christianity a way *from* this world or old aeon *to* a transcendent Kingdom of God. All too naturally the resurrected Christ of faith progressively assumed the form of the celestial redeemer gods of the Hellenistic world, because the resurrection itself was apprehended as a movement to transcendence, and this movement was already established as the foundation of the Hellenistic mystery cults. Accordingly, to worship Jesus as *Kyrios* or Lord is to worship him as a celestial and transcendent Lord.

By this process of development the Kingdom of God became exactly the opposite of what it had been in the proclamation of Jesus. No longer the immanent actualization of a transcendent beyond, it became the transcendent actualization of an immanent here and now. No longer a forward movement from a primordial past to an eschatological future, it became a backward movement from an eschatological present to a primordial and transcendent eternity. No longer the initial and immediate expression of an imminent and total apocalyptic future, it became a spiritual realm which is eternally present. At all these points and others we can see how Christianity inverted and reversed the eschatological proclamation of Jesus, and did so not at its periphery but in its innermost foundation, in its apprehension of the triumphant and resurrected Christ. Ever more decisively the Lord of the Resurrection became a re-embodiment of that transcendent mystery which Jesus had assaulted and reversed, so that Christ himself became in faith the opposite of the Kingdom which Jesus had proclaimed. Not only did the proclaimer become the proclaimed, but this occurred by way of a reversal of the original proclamation!

Is it not clear that the way to the original eschatological ground of faith is by way of an inversion and reversal of the given and established Christ of faith? Without at this point denying the substance of Paul's words that if Christ has not been "raised" then our faith is in vain, we must inquire into the fundamental meaning of "raising" and "resurrection." No doubt Paul's language comes out of the Jewish apocalyptic tradition, a tradition which expected the resurrection of the dead on the last day. For Paul, the resurrected Christ is the "first fruits" of that resurrection, and the resurrected Christ will reign until He has destroyed every authority and power; but the last enemy to be destroyed is death. Then comes the end, when Christ will deliver the Kingdom to God the Father: "When all things are subjected to him, then the Son himself will also be subjected to him who put all things under him, that God may be all in all" (I Corinthians 15:28). We must note that Paul associates the resurrected Christ with a monarchic and even cosmic power, and when that power has been fully exercised all things will be subject to Christ, and then Christ himself will also be "subjected" to the Father. Is it not apparent that Paul identifies the power of the resurrected Christ with the sovereignty of the transcendent Lord?

This is clearly one meaning which Paul apprehends in the resurrected Christ, but we must also seek another. Paul believed that flesh and blood cannot inherit the Kingdom of God, for the perishable cannot inherit the imperishable. Thus when the end comes, the faithful will all be changed in a moment: "For this perishable nature must put on the imperishable, and this mortal nature must put on immortality" (I Corinthians 15:53). Indeed, Paul's vision of the coming resurrection of the dead gives us a clear insight into his understanding of the already resurrected Christ:

> So it is with the resurrection of the dead. What is sown is perishable, what is raised is imperishable. It is sown in dishonor, it is raised in glory. It is sown in weakness, it is raised in power. It is sown a physical body, it is raised a spiritual body. (I Corinthians 15:42ff.)

All of this depends upon Paul's distinction between the "physical" and the "spiritual" body: the physical body is from the earth, and the spiritual body is from Heaven. So it is that the first Adam is of dust, and the second Adam or Christ is of Heaven: "Just as we have borne the image of the man of dust, we shall also bear the image of the man of heaven" (I Corinthians 15:49). While it might not be necessary to judge that Paul established a dualistic distinction between the physical and the spiritual body, he clearly identified the resurrected Christ as a spiritual Lord, and envisioned what he called our Lord Jesus Christ as "the man of heaven."

Say what one will, there is no gainsaying the fact that the first apostle to the gentiles and the earliest writer of the New Testament understood Christ as a monarchic, a spiritual, and a heavenly Lord. This is not to assert that this is the only understanding Paul had of Christ, or that there are not other elements of his understanding which radically conflict with this one; but it is to say that this was an essential ground of Paul's apprehension of Christ, and presumably an essential ground of the faith of the ancient church. Moreover, in Paul's understanding, it was precisely the event of the resurrection which elevated or "raised" Christ. Through the triumph of the resurrection, Christ conquers sin, death, and Satan, and thence inherits his destined mantle of a final spiritual and sovereign power. It is this conjunction of spiritual and sovereign power which seems so strange to us today; and while it doubtless had a basis in Jewish apocalypticism, it must also be judged to be a turning away from Jesus' eschatological proclamation. The very idea that the resurrected Christ is exalted to a heavenly or spiritual realm is a reversal of the movement of the Kingdom which Jesus proclaimed. The forward and downward movement of the Kingdom of God here becomes the backward and upward movement of ascension. Christ returns to Heaven and assumes or resumes the glory and sovereignty of God; and although he only temporarily exercises the sovereignty of God, he does so nonetheless—and not until all things are subject to him will he become subject to the Father.

Paul never actually speaks of the ascension or of the ascended Christ, but his whole manner of understanding the resurrection as the raising or exaltation of Christ to Heaven is a way of affirming the ascension. In the faith of the church, whether ancient or modern, ascension means glorification, a glorification which at bottom means deification, or, at the very least, a cosmic epiphany of the eternal Lordship of Christ. While a clear account of the ascension of Jesus is not to be found in the New Testament—it is recorded in only one of the Gospels, and even this is probably an addition to the original Gospel of Luke—it is nevertheless clear that all the New Testament accounts of the resurrection, just as all its portraits of the exalted and resurrected Christ, follow the symbolic pattern of ascension. It would appear that the ancient church had no other means of understanding the consummation of the work of Jesus. Or, for that matter, no other means of understanding the consummation of the Kingdom of God. Indeed, even when the New Testament speaks of the descent of Christ, it speaks of it as a descent from Heaven, as can be seen in this passage from the Gospel of John: "No one has ascended into heaven but he who descended from heaven, the Son of man" (3:13). To be sure, the ancient church came to believe that Christ descended into Hell, but there is only one extremely obscure reference to this in the New Testament (I Peter 3:18–20). It would seem that the Hellenistic church came to believe in the descent into Hell as a means of understanding how Christ could have mediated salvation to the righteous among the gentile dead. There does not seem to be even the slightest hint in the faith of the ancient church that the descent into Hell could have been the consummation of the work of both Jesus and the Kingdom. Should it not for that very reason all the more attract us?

III ✳

We might pause at this point and reconsider Jesus as a revolutionary prophet and herald of an eschatological and therefore final salvation. If Jesus truly was a revolutionary prophet, then, humanly and historically considered, we should not expect an immediate or rapid acceptance and understanding of his work and message. Until the much later time of Muhammad, who was the first prophet to record his own message, there had been no written account of a major prophet (with the possible exception of Jeremiah) which had been recorded so rapidly after the event as was the New Testament. Remembering that Buddhist scriptures did not come into existence until some five hundred years after the Buddha's death, we will be given a further perspective for evaluating the New Testament. How could the Christian who believes that Jesus is the Christ—and a "light" shining in the "darkness"—believe that his work and message could be fully and truly recorded within a few years after his death? Obviously such a belief is possible only for one who accepts the ecclesiastical dogma of revelation and inspiration, the dogma that the Bible is the Word of God. Many modern Christians moderate this dogma by affirming that the Bible contains or embodies—rather than *is*— the Word of God, but they retain the dogmatic belief that it is finally God who speaks in the Bible. But once this dogma has been renounced, as it must be by anyone who seeks to go beyond the established forms of Christianity, then the New Testament can no longer be accorded a literal or final authority.

How well modern historical and critical biblical scholarship has taught us that the Bible is a human document, or a whole library of widely differing documents, and yet how few Christians there are, including theologians, who seem to be able to surrender the ecclesiastical dogma of inspiration! This becomes apparent when we realize how few Christians believe that anything comparable to revelation or inspiration has occurred after the canonization of the New Testament. Is the Christian to believe that the Christ who came to make all things new came to establish the most dogmatic religion on earth? Nor is there anything new about the Christian dogma of inspiration; we find its counterpart in every other form of priestly or ecclesiastical religion. Priestly religions, which are fundamentally in quest of the sacrality of a primordial past, commonly affirm that the earlier the scripture the fuller and truer the revelation it records. This can be seen in the attitude of Judaism towards the Torah or of Hinduism towards the Vedas. But Christianity by necessity must reverse this priestly form of belief. For it believes in the Christ whom it calls the last of the prophets, just as it believes that the New Testament is a fuller or a higher or a truer revelation than the Old. Moreover, Christianity is grounded in the new, not the old, covenant, even if its ecclesiastical expressions have celebrated the new covenant as a renewal of the old. Above all, Christianity has an eschatological ground, which at the very least means that it is grounded in a movement of revelation and salvation moving from a primordial beginning to a final and eschatological end. Are we to assume that the end was realized with the canonization of the New Testament? Is all subsequent history simply a series of footnotes or commentaries upon the New Testament?

If we are actually to accept the simple thesis that the New Testament is a fully human and historical document, as well as the Christian affirmation that Jesus was a truly new or even revolutionary prophet, then it follows inevitably that the New Testament can contain only an obscure and partial portrait of the Christ who is known in faith as making all things new. At most, the New Testament could be accepted as the initial and provisional record of a revolutionary movement and process of salvation. Since a revolutionary movement is essentially a forward movement, albeit a radical one, it also follows that wherever the New Testament records an earlier or prerevolutionary faith or vision, it reflects a human refusal and reversal of its own intrinsic source. We should expect just such a resistance and opposition to a new and revolutionary process. In fact, were such resistance absent and unknown, we would rightfully suspect the revolutionary identity of the movement. Perhaps it could even be said that the degree to which a movement is actually revolutionary can be measured by the degree to which the movement itself resists and opposes its own revolutionary ground. Whether this is so or not—and if so it illuminates the revolutionary identity of Christianity—we should quite naturally expect to find an inversion and reversal of the eschatological proclamation of Jesus in the New Testament itself. Of course, the New Testament is our only source for the historical Jesus. But as such a large body of modern New Testament scholarship has discovered and demonstrated, it is precisely when a particular event or saying in the Gospels can be known as being most estranged from the life and faith of the early church that it can most clearly be judged to be a true reflection of the acts and proclamation of the historical Jesus. Fortunately, the New Testament is a profoundly offensive book, and wherever it is most offensive to the Christian, we should recognize it as being most faithful to the original and eschatological Jesus.

Thus far theology has paid far too little attention to the forward-moving nature of an eschatological and revolutionary movement. For theology has resisted the fundamental idea that an eschatological movement evolves by

transcending and thus moving beyond or ahead of its previous expressions. If an eschatological movement is a fulfillment of its own past, it is so only inasmuch as it negates its earlier forms and expressions, therein allowing
its own movement to evolve to a new and final form. We
can broaden our understanding of an eschatological
movement by taking up the religious or mythical symbols
of flesh and Spirit. Then we can attempt to understand an
eschatological movement not only as a movement from
past to future but also as a movement from Spirit to flesh.
This is fully in keeping with the fundamental faith of
Christianity, which already in the Gospel of John affirms
that the Word became flesh. Is it possible to apprehend
an eschatological meaning in the Word's becoming flesh?
But this is to inquire if the Christ of faith is an eschatological Christ. The mere posing of this question should
lead us to see the necessity of employing the symbolic
language of flesh and Spirit so as to unveil yet another
meaning of the realization or actualization of the Kingdom of God.

Previously we attempted to understand the dawning of
the Kingdom of God both as an immanent actualization
of a transcendent beyond, and as the initial and immediate expression of an imminent and total future. Is it possible within this pattern of meaning to arrive at an eschatological understanding of resurrection or of the resurrected
Christ or Jesus? If it is possible to do so, then it becomes
necessary to forswear all ancient or pre-eschatological language about the movement from flesh to Spirit; or, at most,

to employ it only negatively. Paul clearly employs pre-eschatological language in his discussion of the meaning of
resurrection (e.g., "the man of heaven"). Thus for the most
part he imputes an ancient mythical meaning to an eschatological and final event. Can we invert or reverse Paul's understanding and thereby arrive at an eschatological meaning of an eschatological event? To do so we would have to
say that, eschatologically envisioned, resurrection is not a
movement from flesh to Spirit, but is rather in some sense a
movement from Spirit to flesh. But in what sense? Certainly
not literally; but this does not mean that we must abandon
the imagery of ascent and descent.

Let us first be fully aware that if we are to arrive at a
truly eschatological understanding of resurrection, then
we must be prepared to negate and annul the ancient
mythical meaning of resurrection. Already we have come
to the realization that the ascending movement from flesh
to Spirit is a return to a primordial form of Spirit. Therefore it is a reversal of the forward and final movement of
an eschatological process. Can we now say that an eschatological movement of resurrection would be a *descending* movement from the "higher" level of Spirit to the
"lower" level of flesh? This would mark an attempt to
speak theologically about a divine movement from the
"higher" form of Spirit to the "lower" form of flesh. In
other words, it would be an attempt to understand resurrection as incarnation, as the Word's becoming flesh.
Here, the descending movement from Spirit to flesh
would also be an eschatological movement from a pri-

mordial form of Spirit to an eschatological form of flesh. Yet such a mode of understanding would eschew all traditional theological efforts to maintain and preserve the original or primordial nature of God when speaking of the incarnation. On the contrary, it would insist that the divine process can undergo the eschatological movement of resurrection only insofar as it negates and transcends its own primordial and transcendent ground. Thereby the divine process itself passes into a new identity and form: it is "resurrected."

Can we reach an eschatological understanding of the resurrected Christ by inverting and reversing the ancient church's apprehension of the movement of resurrection and ascension? All too significantly the ancient church identified the movement of resurrection with the movement of ascension, thereby reaching its faith in Christ as the ascended and exalted Lord, the Christ of glory who is the celestial and monarchic Cosmocrator. From a consistently eschatological point of view, the Christ of glory can be seen to be a consequence of ancient Christianity's transforming the forward and downward movement of the Kingdom into the upward and backward movement of the ascension. But what if a radical faith were to transform the backward and upward movement of the ascension into the downward and forward movement of the Word's becoming flesh? Then faith could affirm that the resurrected Christ is *not* the Christ of glory—not the exalted and celestial Christ, not the monarchic Cosmocrator, not "the man of heaven," and not the primordial

Logos or Word. Quite the contrary: the resurrected Christ remains and *is* yet more deeply the Christ of passion, the lowly and suffering Christ, the servant and the slave, "the man of dust," the eschatological or final Word.

At this point these inverted images can do little to point to a reverse identity of Christ; but they illustrate the vital importance of negating an inherited religious imagery, just as they point to the theological significance of the symbolic movements of up and down. If the resurrection were understood as the consequence of a downward and forward movement of incarnation, then we could apprehend the divine process as passing from a past to a future form or mode *in* the resurrection. Then the downward movement of descent would appear as the forward movement of an eschatological realization. Just as the ancient church envisioned the consummation of the work of Jesus and the Kingdom through the images of ascension and glorification, we should strive to envision that consummation through images of descent and humiliation. As opposed to exaltation and glorification, self-giving or self-negation here becomes the primary image, not only of the way, but also of the goal or destiny of Christ. No longer would resurrection be envisioned as a transition to a heavenly and transcendent "spiritual body," but rather as a movement from the transcendent realm of Spirit to the immanent realm of flesh, and hence as a transition to an earthly and immediate "physical body." Then we would be given another way to an understanding of a divine and eschatological movement of negation and reversal. For in negating and dissolving its transcendent ground, the divine movement would reverse its primordial identity as Spirit, thereby releasing itself in a final and immanent form as flesh.

The negation and emptying of transcendence could then be envisioned as the passage or transition of Spirit into flesh. The Word becomes flesh only by negating and reversing its original and primordial form as Spirit. When the primordial and transcendent ground of the divine process is inverted and reversed, then the divine process itself becomes actualized or realized as immanence or flesh. Symbolically speaking, this is no more and no less than a means of understanding or envisioning the resurrection of Christ as the descent into Hell. Otherwise stated, this is a way of negating and reversing everything which Christianity has understood as the Christ of glory. Hence it is an attempt to negate the ancient religious form and identity of Christianity. Orthodox Christianity presents itself as a fulfillment of the religious yearning of humanity for a primordial form of Spirit. It is an answer to an ancient longing for the beyond, for Heaven; thus the Christ of orthodox Christianity is the Christ of Heaven. Not only does orthodox Christianity believe that the resurrection of Christ was his triumphant ascension into Heaven, but it also believes that Heaven is the abode of Christ until the end of time, and that Heaven is the final destiny of all who truly live in Christ. Yet have we not long since learned that all such ideas and images are as far removed as possible from the original proclamation of Jesus? Then is there a clearer or more decisive route to an eschatological Christ than the obvious way of inverting and reversing everything which orthodox Christianity has named and envisioned as Heaven? Is not the way which we seek a way which can only be manifest to us as a descent into Hell?

IV ✳

Heaven and Hell are, of course, symbolic or mythical categories, and when they assume a literal meaning they can no longer serve as vehicles for the language of either theology or faith. Nevertheless, their symbolic meaning is of great importance. Within this schema or pattern of meaning, it is impossible to dissociate Heaven and Hell from the imagery of higher and lower or up and down or above and below. Heaven is intrinsically a symbol of a transcendent realm, of a distant and exalted sphere; it is associated with images of mountains, the sky, and the heavens. As opposed to everything which is manifest as being immediately actual and real, Heaven evokes a nostalgia or yearning for the beyond, a distant region free of the pain and turbulence of this world, and above all free of suffering and death. We can most easily understand the symbolic name of Heaven by conceiving it as the absolute negation of the here and now; hence it is another world, the hereafter, a world of infinite and eternal bliss. Light and darkness have also been primary images of

Heaven and Hell; the intrinsic opposition between darkness and light long serving as a symbolic image of the impassable chasm dividing Hell from Heaven. Symbolically speaking, Hell is not simply other than Heaven. It is its inherent and intrinsic opposite: the realm of chaos, of suffering, and of death.

But we must not lose sight of the fundamental imagery of high and low and up and down. Heaven is "high," it is up there; it is above and beyond. Hell, on the contrary, is "low," it is down below; or, it is beyond only inasmuch as it is the "center" of earth. Nor is it accidental that Hell became literally understood as the center of the earth, for Heaven and earth are contraries or opposites in a vast body of mythical imagery. What should strike us as particularly significant is that the center of earth became the object of a religious terror and dread, and nowhere did this occur so powerfully as in the Christian world. Hell is the underworld, it is "below" the earth; or, more truly understood, it is the embodiment or center of the chaos, the darkness, the turbulence, and the pain of earth. Thus it is the realm of the dead, of the "spiritually" dead, and Hell itself becomes envisioned as eternal death, just as Heaven had been envisioned as eternal life. The realm of eternal or ultimate death is of necessity the opposite of the transcendent realm. For only the loss of Heaven makes possible a transition to Hell. Consequently, to move from Heaven to Hell is not only to move from eternal life to eternal death but also to move from pure transcendence to its opposite.

Pre-exilic Israel had neither an idea nor a symbol of eternal life or eternal death. Thus it knew little or nothing of what Christianity was later to know as Heaven and Hell. The Christian symbols of Heaven and Hell, at least in their original and New Testament form, are the product of Jewish apocalypticism. Here, Heaven and Hell are apprehended as the Kingdom of God and its opposite; or, as old aeon and new aeon, old creation and new creation, flesh and Spirit. But apocalypticism brought a new meaning to death. Death now becomes the correlate of the apocalyptic and eschatological symbol of the end; the end of the world is the death of the old creation or old aeon, the eternal death of a fallen form of the world and time. What must be emphasized here is that the eternal life of the new aeon or new creation is inseparably related to the eternal death of the old. Apart from the ultimate or final end of the old creation or old aeon, the new aeon must remain both unrealized and unreal. Moreover, the advent of eternal death, or the coming of the end of the world, is but the reverse side of the advent of the Kingdom of God. Therefore faith must pass through the end or death of the old aeon to participate in the new and final reality of the Kingdom of God.

Now an interior passage through the reality of death becomes the way of salvation, a way which reached its eschatological consummation in Christianity. Already in Paul we find the continually repeated formula that it is only by dying and rising again with Christ that we can enter the Kingdom of God. Paul understood this dying and rising again with Christ as a real "co-experiencing" (Schweitzer's word) of Jesus' death and resurrection. Granting that Paul's is an eschatological or resurrection mysticism, as Schweitzer insists, is it possible to detach Paul's eschatological understanding of faith as a dying with Christ from Paul's pre-eschatological understanding of immortality as eternal life? That is to say, is it possible to understand eschatological faith as a dying with Christ which culminates in a downward and forward movement of resurrection? Indeed, is a way to this possibility established by understanding the resurrection not as a passage to eternal life but rather as a movement from eternal life to "eternal death"? Eternal death, in this sense, so far from being a merely literal death, would be identical with the final and eschatological death of the crucifixion. Then we could realize that the descent into Hell is the symbolic equivalent of the incarnation and the crucifixion.

Eternal death could then appear as yet another symbol of that pure immanence which is the opposite of pure transcendence. Just as we attempted to understand pure immanence as the consequence of an eschatological negation and reversal of pure transcendence, so now we must likewise attempt to understand eternal death as the actualization of an eschatological negation and reversal of eternal life. Once again a dualistic understanding must be resolutely avoided; that is, any understanding of Heaven and Hell or eternal life and eternal death as eternal and unchanging opposites. We must seek an eternal life which can be understood or envisioned as becoming eternal death, just as we must seek an eternal death which can be known as an ultimate and final event. Death now becomes the all-important symbol. Accordingly, we must center attention upon the image of death, seeking to apprehend eternal death as a comprehensive symbol of the emptying of Heaven. Hell must now appear as the full and total opposite of Heaven. That is to say, the emptying of Heaven must not be understood in a literal or dualistic sense, but rather understood as the negation and reversal of the transcendence of Heaven. Eternal death is an eschatological consequence of negating and reversing the distance and the beyondness of Heaven. Only when Heaven has been emptied of Spirit can eternal life be actualized as eternal death. Only when the divine process has been emptied of primordial Spirit can Heaven be realized as flesh or Hell.

The form of this process or movement of Heaven into Hell or Spirit into flesh would be identical with the form of the movement from transcendence into immanence. Just as an eschatological immanence re-embodies in a reverse form a primordial transcendence, so an eschatological flesh or Hell re-embodies in an inverted form a primordial Spirit or Heaven. Furthermore, in each case, the movement is realized only by virtue of an actual act or process of negation and reversal. In speaking of the descent of the Word into flesh or of Heaven into Hell, the act or event which releases this movement is symbolically known as death, and as an eternal death at that. Is it possible to understand Jesus' eschatological proclamation as being centered upon such a symbol of death? Not merely in the sense in which traditional apocalypticism was grounded in the coming of the end of the world, but in the far deeper sense that the dawning of the Kingdom of God ushers in the end of the eternal life of God Himself. Here, the dawning of the Kingdom of God would not only bring about the death of all previous images and symbols of the Word, but would also incorporate the end of the life of Heaven. The dawning of the Kingdom of God would be the movement of Word into flesh, the descent of Heaven into Hell.

If the dawning of the Kingdom demands that all attention be turned from the transcendent and the beyond to the immediate and the here and now, could we not say that such an eschatological situation reflects the dying of Spirit and its resurrection as flesh or Hell? When the death of Spirit is understood as effecting or embodying the dissolution and emptying of all transcendent and primordial forms of Spirit, then the resurrection can be envisioned as bringing about a truly new or eschatological creation. Flesh as the new creation? Yes, but not in the sense that the flesh of the old creation or old aeon becomes manifest as Spirit, but rather in the sense that the Spirit of the old aeon is reversed in such a manner as finally to give it the form and identity of flesh. This whole mode of approach could lead us to the realization that the dawning of the Kingdom of God is the initial expression and embodiment of the Word's becoming flesh and

of Heaven's becoming Hell. Jesus, in his acts and his proclamation, is not only the herald of the Kingdom and of
Hell, but also their embodiment, their own inherent and
immediate expression. The ancient church reversed the
eschatological identity of the Kingdom of God and apprehended it as the advent of transcendent and primordial
power. Then the victory or the resurrection of Christ appears as the glorification or even deification of Jesus. The
Kingdom of God becomes manifest as the Kingdom of
Heaven, and the resurrected Jesus appears as a celestial
and transcendent Lord. But if once again we invert and
reverse the faith of the ancient church, then we can apprehend the resurrected Jesus as the embodiment of both
the emptying of Heaven and the final negation of transcendent Spirit.

Here, the crucifixion is not a death which actualizes a
transition from flesh to Spirit, but, on the contrary, a
death which is the fulfillment of a movement from Spirit
to flesh. What dies in Jesus is the transcendent form of
Spirit, and what is resurrected in Jesus is a new and final
mode of flesh. From this point of view, it is of vital importance, symbolically, to apprehend the passion and
death of Jesus as culminating not in an eternal life or
Heaven but rather in an eternal death or Hell. In the
Christian tradition, as opposed to the Orient, Heaven and
Hell are ultimate symbols; they evoke a vision of an ultimate destiny and identity. Thus the Jesus who appears as
the man of Heaven is the Jesus who is affirmed by faith as
the ultimate and final Christ. Then the finality of Christ

becomes the finality of Heaven, and Heaven becomes the final or eschatological identity of everyone who lives in Christ. The way of life then becomes the way of "life," of eternal life, of Heaven. Yet what would it mean to affirm, on the contrary, that the way of Christ is the way of "death," of eternal death, of Hell? At the very least it would mean that Jesus is "the man of Hell," the one in whom an eternal death is actualized, a death embodying the death of eternal life. Just as the man of Heaven embodies eternal life, so the man of Hell embodies eternal death. In neither case do life and death preserve their given or original identities: for to live in the Christ of Heaven is to live in primordial Spirit, and to live in the Christ of Hell is to live in a new and eschatological flesh. And just as the epiphany of Christ in Heaven evokes the final destiny of all who live in Spirit, so the descent of Christ into Hell evokes the final destiny of all who live in the inherent and intrinsic opposite of Spirit, of all who live in eternal death or Hell.

V ✳

When we give an eschatological identity to the ancient Christian symbol of the Word's becoming flesh, then we can apprehend the dawning of the Kingdom of God as the descent and incarnation of a spiritual and transcendent Word or Heaven. The acts and words of Jesus can then be understood as not simply pointing to the dawning of the Kingdom, but as being themselves expressions of the Kingdom, embodiments of its own movement and direction. Initially, the Kingdom is realized in its proclamation; it is expressed in the work of its proclaimer. Is it possible, however, from this point of view, to understand that Jesus himself is in some sense the content of his own proclamation? That is to say, if the proclaimer became the proclaimed in ancient or primitive Christianity, is it possible to reverse the ancient Christ of faith, the Christ of glory, and by this means unveil a new and eschatological Christ, a Christ who is identical with the Word of a fully eschatological proclamation? If the proclamation of Jesus is itself the incarnation of an eschatological Word, can we understand that Word as being embodied in the life and death of Jesus? Is the original Word of Jesus finally identical with the Christ of a fully eschatological faith?

Jesus points to a Kingdom in process even now of emptying and reversing its own transcendent power and identity. As that power is emptied and reversed, it passes into an immanent and immediate form, and dawns here and now at the center of time and flesh. Already we have observed that such an eschatological movement is possible only as a consequence of a negation and reversal of a transcendent ground. Now we must come to see that the fulfillment or consummation of a purely eschatological movement can only be in death, in the eternal death of a transcendent eternity. If it is now possible to see that the Kingdom of Heaven and the Christ of Heaven are inversions and reversals of Jesus' eschatological proclamation, is it also possible to see that Jesus' proclamation could only be fulfilled through his own movement into Hell or eternal death? Then we could see that the passion and death of Jesus are the inevitable consummation of an eschatological movement of descent and incarnation. In no sense whatsoever, then, may the crucifixion of Jesus be regarded as the portal to eternal life or as the way to Heaven. Quite to the contrary, in Jesus, death becomes its own end and goal. In him, and through his death, death becomes eternal as the descent into Hell.

If ancient Christianity envisioned Christ as ascending ever higher into Heaven, we must envision Jesus as descending ever deeper into Hell. Eternal death or Hell is his final destiny, and not as its passive and impotent victim, but rather as a consequence of the Word which he embodied and proclaimed. Just as the Christian dies with Christ and therein co-experiences the passion and the crucifixion, so we must be led to realize that Jesus fully dies his own death, and dies in such a way as to make his death his destiny. His death is not simply a death, nor even simply his own death; for it appears in faith as an ultimate and final event, as an eschatological consummation. Therefore the death of Jesus is an eternal death, the final death of the eternal life of Spirit. His death is the initial and immediate fulfillment of the eschatological movement of the Word's becoming flesh, of the descent of Heaven or Spirit into Hell. It is precisely because the death of Jesus is an eternal death that it culminates in the descent into Hell. Now Hell becomes the truest symbol of

Spirit, the truest symbol of that resurrected Spirit which has passed through an eternal death so as fully and finally to become flesh.

Not only does Spirit descend and die in Jesus, but in his death the eternal death of Spirit is realized as self-dis-solution or self-negation. Through his death, and through its finality, the emptying of Spirit appears as self-empty-ing. Here, the heavens are darkened and emptied of Spirit, but they are finally darkened by that self-emptying which Spirit itself ultimately realizes in the death of Jesus. It is just because the death of Jesus is an actual and real event that it can be the expression of the actual self-negation of Spirit. But it is so only inasmuch as it is a final or eternal death, the culmination of the work or movement of the Kingdom which Jesus proclaimed. Now the movement of the Kingdom is fully manifest as a downward movement or as a descent into Hell. The escha-tological symbol of the descent into Hell unveils the finality of the crucifixion. But the finality of the crucifixion makes the dawning of the Kingdom manifest as the self-emptying or self-negation of God. Only death actualizes this final self-negation of God, and thus the death of Jesus fully actual-izes the eschatological negation and self-reversal of Spirit.

Eternal death is the purest eschatological image of the Kingdom of God. Only the fullness and finality of death finally release the Kingdom of God in the immediacy and the actuality of the here and the now. Thus eternal death is the symbolic name of the goal of an eschatological movement of self-negation. When transcendence passes through a full eschatological movement of self-negation and self-reversal, eternal life passes into eternal death, and Heaven itself becomes manifest as Hell. Heaven is finally emptied through eternal death, and thereby Spirit fully passes into its own inherent opposite. Not only does transcendent and primordial power turn into its own opposite in eternal death, but the distance and beyondness of transcendence are immediately actualized here and now. Yet the very reversal of transcendence actualizes the eternity and bliss of Heaven in the finality and immediacy of death. In the descent into Hell, the Word fully and finally becomes flesh, and fully becomes flesh by emptying itself of Spirit. Consequently, it is the self-emptying of Spirit which creates a new and eschatological flesh, a flesh freed of every sign and memory of Spirit. It is just this final flesh which fully realizes the reversal and self-negation of transcendence; thus the finality of death is the innermost goal of the Kingdom of God.

Hell is not only the opposite of Heaven; it is the opposite of that pure Spirit which is identical with Heaven. Thus Hell is the necessary and inevitable goal of the self-negation of transcendence. While Hell, quite simply, is eternal death, it becomes manifest as eternal death only as a consequence of the reversal or emptying of Heaven. Therefore the advent or dawning of Hell does not simply mean the death of eternity or Heaven. It far rather means the epiphany of Heaven as Hell, of eternal life as eternal death. In fully and finally becoming flesh, the Word does not simply negate its original form: it reverses the primordial transcendence of Spirit, so that Spirit itself actually passes into flesh. If Hell is the final name of Spirit, it is a name which can be reached only by passing through the death of Spirit, the eternal death of everything which is manifest as "high" and beyond. Not only must everything which is manifest as beyond become manifest as Hell. But the descent of Christ or Spirit into Hell must actualize the beyond as eternal death, as the fullness of a transcendent eternity is absorbed in the immediacy and finality of death.

4

The
Contemporary
Christ

✳

1 ✳

Christianity has always posed the overwhelming and seemingly unanswerable question of how
the individual historical Jesus can be the universal Christ
of faith. Perhaps the earliest answer to this question, and
one that has always been present whether implicitly or
explicitly throughout the history of Christian theology, is
the Pauline affirmation that the individual Jesus becomes
the universal Christ through the final events of the crucifixion and the resurrection. This position is, however,
apparently at odds with the orthodox dogma that the
eternal Word or Spirit is fully present in Jesus even from
the time of his conception and birth. From the time of
Nicea, orthodox Christianity has affirmed that Jesus
Christ is fully God and fully man. But this affirmation has
not resolved, even for Christian orthodoxy, the primary
question of the identities of Jesus and of Christ. This pe-
rennial Christian question can be phrased in Pauline language by asking what is the relationship between the

135

Jesus of the old aeon and the Christ of the new aeon? Or, between the Jesus who is manifest in the flesh and the Jesus who is manifest in the Spirit? Or, calling upon modern language, what is the relationship between the Jesus who is known objectively and historically and the Christ who is known only in faith?

We must remember that what we commonly take for granted as historical thinking and understanding came into existence only at the time of the European Enlightenment. Only since that time have historical figures and events stood out in their own contingent singularity and uniqueness. Therefore it is only in the modern world that one can discover a conscious awareness of the vast distance separating an earlier from a later time. It is just this awareness which lies behind the modern Christian's sense of estrangement from Jesus, an estrangement which was deepened profoundly by the modern discovery of the eschatological identity of the historical Jesus. Since the time of Kierkegaard it has been common in modern theological thinking to establish a dichotomy between the historical Jesus and the Christ of faith. While it has been challenged repeatedly, such a dichotomy would seem to be essential to any form of modern Christianity seeking to preserve both what we can know as the historical Jesus and what has been given to faith as the universal Christ. For there would seem to be no way from the singularity and particularity of the historical Jesus to that universality which the Christian apprehends in the Christ who is the source of salvation and life.

Or is there? Already Paul envisioned a resurrected Christ who is a new Christ, a Christ of the new aeon or new creation; and the new creation is manifest, or is actual and real, only because the form or schema of the old creation is passing away. Furthermore, the new Christ is a consequence of the historical Jesus. For it is only through the passion and death of the original Jesus that the resurrection occurs and the new age is decisively and finally established. Here, it is the actual suffering and death of Jesus which occasions or embodies the resurrection, and apart from that suffering and death there could have been no resurrection and no triumph of the new age. Paul went so far as to establish a dichotomy, or so it would appear, between the fleshly Jesus and the resurrected Christ—insisting that faith is directed only towards the resurrected Christ, only to the new and not to the old Jesus. Does this mean that faith is directed only toward the Christ of glory? Within a Pauline mode of understanding, the answer to this question must be both yes and no: yes, in the sense that it is only the resurrected Christ who is the object of faith, but no in the sense that the resurrected Christ is impossible and unreal apart from the passion and death of the original Jesus. But mustn't this mean that the individual death of Jesus is an essential ground of the universal or eschatological Christ of faith?

While it may not be possible to say that the individual selfhood of Jesus is essential to the resurrection—for modern New Testament scholarship has all but dissolved what little remains in the Gospels of the personal individuality of Jesus—it is necessary to say that the individual death of Jesus is essential to the resurrection. Can we speak of his death as being singular and unique? It certainly was so in terms of its impact upon history. But is there any way present to us which can lead us to the singularity and uniqueness of Jesus' own suffering and death? First, we must note that there is a unique quality present in the Christian way of dying and rising again with Christ. As opposed to the fertility and mystery deities of the Greek, Near Eastern, and Hellenistic worlds, the Christian Christ is inseparable from a human and historical individual. Accordingly, a Christian dying with Christ is a dying at a unique and individual Calvary, even if Christianity did absorb many of the mythical and ritual patterns of alien ways of salvation. Truly to die with Christ is to co-experience the individual death of Jesus. And the memory of that individual death has either vanished from history or it is present in a uniquely Christian way of faith.

Once granted the historical complexity of Christianity, is it possible to speak of a uniquely Christian way of faith? Are there not a number of Christian ways of faith, and do not these appear, and reappear, and disappear once again, with startling multiformity throughout the course of Christian history? No doubt all this is true. But if we could discover a Christian way of faith which is singular and unique insofar as it stands at the greatest possible distance from non-Christian ways of salvation and freedom, then we may well be given by this means a path into the unique and individual death of Jesus. Indeed, doesn't Paul's formula of dying and rising again with Christ already point out such a path to a uniquely Christian way of faith? For Christianity, and Christianity alone, celebrates the concrete and factual actuality of death as the way to salvation. Underlying the Christian celebration of the crucifixion and the resurrection is a new openness to death as an ultimately real and yet final event. Nowhere else is death given its simple if brutal actuality, for nowhere else in history has man found salvation and release through the human event of death.

While there is nothing singular or unique in Paul's understanding of the resurrected Lord as "the man of Heaven," there is nothing elsewhere in the history of religions comparable to Paul's celebration of the individual and historical events of the crucifixion and the resurrection as the sole source of salvation. To judge by his letters, Paul was only interested in Jesus' death and resurrection; for he paid no attention to Jesus as a prophet, a teacher, or a moral example. This is one reason why so many scholars have identified Paul as the founder of Christianity; for it would appear that he has simply transposed the historical Jesus into a Hellenistic mystery god, and ignored everything in Jesus which did not fit into the already established patterns of the mystery religions. But the fact remains that Paul apprehends the crucifixion and the resurrection as being in some sense individual historical events, and there was no precedent for this in previous religious traditions; just as there was no real precedent for believing that a genuine historical figure of any kind is a savior and redeemer. Buddhism presents an instructive contrast to Christianity at this point: the deified Buddhas of Mahayana Buddhism are wholly detached from the historical figure, Siddhartha Gautama. Only in Christianity is an incarnate Word or Spirit apprehended as being fully actual and present in a concrete individual. Yet here that Word most decisively appears in the unique and individual death of Jesus.

When we recall that the resurrected Christ of ancient Christianity is the celestial and monarchic Christ of glory, there is certainly nothing in the image of the resurrection alone which is singular and unique—except insofar as Christianity went beyond other religions in exalting the power and the glory of Christ. It is rather the image of death which takes us into the center of a uniquely Christian way. Jesus not only fully realized his work and proclamation in his death; but in his death he wholly died to everything which was individually and particularly himself. It is not accidental that the writers and editors of the New Testament were so little interested in the individuality and particularity of Jesus. True, mythical forms the world over have an almost inevitable tendency to strip historical events of their factual and contingent actuality. But modern scholarship has taught us that we know more about Jeremiah and Socrates than we do about Jesus. Moreover, we know far more about the social and political situations of the ancient prophets, for the recorded words of Jesus have no reference to social or political conditions of any kind (even his saying about Caesar could be applied to any ruler in the world). If an eschatological faith is fully realized in Jesus, it is realized in such a manner as to lead to the absolute negation of everything which is humanly and historically his own.

Everything, that is, but his death; for only in his death is the original Jesus still present in history, and only in his dying did he become an individual model for faith. Therefore faith rightly repudiates the "fleshly" Jesus or the "old" Jesus or even Jesus as an individual human being. If the only Jesus who is present to faith is the resurrected Jesus, then the only human image which we can have of Jesus is the image of death, and Jesus becomes for us an eternal Jesus only inasmuch as he is realized as eternal death. Death should be our only image of Jesus, and it is not accidental that we have known him primarily by way of images of the crucifixion—for the crucified Jesus is the only Jesus who can be present at the center of faith. If it is true that it was by way of images of resurrection such an "arising" to celestial glory that Christianity originally betrayed its founder, then we can return to Jesus only by inverting all such imagery and symbolism. But we can never return to the original Jesus, never know or envision the man whom his disciples knew; for that Jesus died on the cross. He is present nowhere but in his death; yet his death is an eternal death and thus is present wherever death is fully actualized and is immediately and finally real.

II ✳

The resurrected Christ who is the embodiment of the
eternal death of Jesus is the Christ who has descended
into Hell. Hell is the point or arena where Christ is present
in the world, and Christ is actual for us only insofar as we
are open to eternal death. What can it mean to speak of
eternal death in the modern world? Is it even possible for
us to speak of an eternal as opposed to a literal or contingent death? First, we should note that it is far easier for us
to speak of an eternal death than of an eternal life. Death
has become a total image for the modern imagination, total
because it draws into itself all that aspiration and hope
which once were bestowed upon the image of eternal life.
Thus death lies at the center of the modern imagination,
and not death as a literal event, but rather a fullness and
finality of death whose presence releases a new energy and
vision. So far from being a mode of entry to eternal life,
death has become for us its own end and goal. In those moments when we are open to the presence of the Christ who
has descended into Hell, eternal death appears to us with
the fullness and finality of what was once manifest to the
Christian as the Kingdom and the Spirit.

Death has always been a total symbol in apocalyptic
and eschatological faith. Apart from the actualization of
the totality of death or the end, there can be no new creation or new aeon, just as apart from the full and final
death of Jesus there can be no new or eschatological

Christ. The Christ of eschatological faith appears only where there is the presence of a full and total death, only where life itself is manifest under the form of death. If the fullness of the Word or Spirit is present in the eternal death of Jesus, then this very fullness must be a consequence of the death or "end" of Spirit. Wherever a primordial and transcendent form of Word or Spirit is negated and reversed, there, declares a radical and eschatological faith, lies the true presence of the "resurrected" Christ. For the resurrected Christ who is a consequence of the descent into Hell can be the embodiment only of the self-negation or self-dissolution of Spirit. But do we not inherit a whole history, indeed, the history of Christendom, in which transcendence has ever more fully darkened or vanished? Has not this dissolution and darkening of transcendence occurred in the concrete actuality of our consciousness and experience? Is it not possible to say that we have been given a history in which a pure and primordial transcendence has descended ever more deeply into Hell or death? A contemporary and radical faith affirms that the descent into Hell has been realized in what we have been given in our world as the history of consciousness and experience. The Christ who is the Lord of our history is the Lord of death: the death of every form of the transcendent and the beyond, the eternal death of the eternal life of Spirit.

Certainly the Christian who believes that Christ is the Lord of history must acknowledge that Christ is the source of what has fully and finally been actualized in our history as the death of God. Is it possible, then, to speak of the eternal death of Jesus as the initial and individual expression of the death of God? May we then affirm that as a consequence of this original eternal death, the death of God has ever more pervasively and comprehensively been realized throughout the whole or universal body of humanity? If the Kingdom of God has triumphed in the fullness of history, must not that triumph take the form of the ever more comprehensive historical realization of the end or death of God? Has not history itself become the arena and the expression of the negation and dissolution of primordial and transcendent Spirit? While these questions resist all cursory answers, they nevertheless point to the most awesome questions facing the individual Christian today. What meaning has the death of God or the dissolution of transcendence for our individual identities? What effect has it already had, whether implicitly or explicitly, upon our individual selfhoods? Is Christ present for us and in us at those points at which we pass through a dissolution of transcendence?

We can begin to take up these questions by addressing ourselves to the problem of authority—particularly the problem of religious authority, the question of absolute or ultimate authority. Nothing is more distinctive about the message and ministry of Jesus than its violent assault upon all given or established forms of authority, whether these be of a religious, a social, or a domestic kind. Not only does he assault all pre-established forms of authority, but the radical thrust of his eschatological proclamation places in question every form of human and social authority. In the words of the Jewish New Testament scholar, Joseph Klausner: "To adopt the teaching of Jesus is to remove oneself from the whole sphere of ordered national and human existence." Not only does his teaching remove its hearer from the sphere of ordered existence, but his acts and words have the effect of dissolving any awareness of such a sphere. Every form of order and authority here stands revealed as being grounded in that old aeon or old creation which even now is passing away. True, Jesus is reported to have taught as one who had "authority"; but his teaching brought an end to all previous authority, even including that of the Torah itself. There perishes in Jesus every form of authority addressed to man from beyond or from without.

Yes, a radical demand is present in Jesus' proclamation, a demand far more radical than any previously present in the prophetic tradition. Yet it comes to its hearer from within the dawning Kingdom, and not from a distant sphere beyond and apart. It is precisely because the Kingdom is dawning here and now that its call and demand assumes a totally immediate and radical form. For this very reason a fully eschatological faith must repudiate traditional moral language. Above all, it must negate and transcend the language and form of the moral imperative. The authority of a moral imperative depends upon a distinction between the "is" and the "ought," between the state of things as they actually are and the state of things as they should or ought to be. There can be no such distinction in a fully eschatological situation, because here the form of this world or the "is" is passing away. When all attention is centered upon the immediate dawning of the Kingdom of God, there can be no awareness of a distinction between the "is" and the "ought." Not only will there be no tension or opposition between the "is" and the "ought," or the indicative and the imperative, but no awareness of an imperative as opposed to an indicative. Here, the "is" and the "ought" pass into each other. Or, rather, each is so radically negated in its prior and given form, that neither can appear and be real in its own inherent and individual identity.

With the disappearance of the indicative and the imperative, the world ceases to be given or eternal, and the Kingdom of God ceases to be distant and apart. Where world *was* in its given or original form, there *is* the Kingdom of God. Where old aeon *was* in its power and authority, there *is* the new aeon or the eschatological Christ. Wherever a given authority now places its call and demand upon us, there arises an occasion for death, for a death inaugurating the freedom of the new aeon or new creation. But this freedom appears and is real only through the actuality of death, only through the actual death of a given form of authority. Until the Kingdom has finally been consummated, this death fully occurs only within the faith of those who live in eternal death, and not yet within the realm of principalities and powers. In the eyes of faith the dawning of the Kingdom has already stripped these powers and principalities of all authority.

It is just when these now darkened powers make their claim for greatest obedience that faith can die to their authority, embodying in its own loss of obedience the death of imperative authority. Wherever an imperative arises or establishes its claim, an eschatological faith must die to both the form and the reality of authority. Not only must it die to the demand of the imperative, but it must die in such a way as to annul the authority of its demand, thereby erasing every sanction associated with the authority of the imperative.

Such a way of faith should not be identified as a simple anarchism. Of course, it is a product of the prophetic tradition, and that tradition in its reform or radical expression had always been anarchistic. Prophetic anarchism, however, it not a simple denial of law and authority. It is rather a defiance and reversal of a given authority, and in its eschatological form it finally engages in an absolute reversal of the authority which it opposes. Jesus not only attacked the rich and the powerful, the pious and the righteous, the strong and the wise. He also assaulted them in such a way as to reveal the foolishness of their wisdom, the weakness of their strength, the guilt of their righteousness, the impiety of their piety, the powerlessness of their power, and the poverty of their wealth. So it is that an eschatological faith seeks out the apparent fullness of the life about it, seeking to apprehend that life as death, so that the Kingdom might be realized or actualized in its midst. It could even be said that wherever the world presents itself as being most powerful and real, there an eschatological judgment of death is most called for, and there an eschatological way of eternal death is most fully called to die to the life and power which it confronts. Only this passage of life into death realizes the presence of the Kingdom of God, so that wherever death is not fully actual and real, there the Kingdom has not yet fully appeared.

An eschatological faith inevitably embodies a judgment of death, an absolute assault upon the givenness of the world which it confronts. Here, one principle clearly stands out: it is the center of power which must be assaulted, the most absolute and sacred authority which must be annulled and dissolved. Accordingly, Jesus does not simply demand obedience. He rather seeks out all those forms of life and power which are most turned away from the dawning Kingdom, and by assaulting their authority and power he realizes the Kingdom in their midst. Or, rather, the Kingdom realizes itself in him insofar as his action and proclamation reverse the world's identity and power. Obviously Jesus did not engage in a physical, or military, or political attack upon the powers of this world. But he brought an end to their authority, that is to their sacred or ultimate authority. By this means he made possible a dissolution of all sacred and transcendent authority, a stilling of every absolute or transcendent claim. Thus it could be said that wherever an eschatological faith is bound to a transcendent or absolute authority, it has reversed the life and death of Jesus. Wherever it is aware of a holy or primordial sanction, it has annulled an eschatological judgment of death. Wherever it is conscious of the "ought" or the imperative, it has resisted the presence of the Kingdom, and is therefore subject to a transient and empty authority which even now is passing away.

III ✳

An all too tempting resolution of the problem of the meaning of eschatological faith for the contemporary believer is given by those theologians who affirm that the coming of the Kingdom of God brings an end to all idolatry and all religion. Religion is here understood to be a human and idolatrous seeking after the presence of the hidden and inaccessible God. God is God and man is man, and an eschatological judgment is a final judgment upon any human attempt to cross the infinite distance separating the creature from the Creator. An eschatological faith frees man from all idolatry, therein restoring humanity to its original and prefallen condition. For when man truly allows God to be God, then man can be simply and only a man. By this means mystery and transcendence are banished from the world and returned to their true source in the absolutely transcendent Creator. From this point of view, an eschatological faith is the essential ground as well as the historical source of modern secular culture and society. Only when faith is directed solely to the total transcendence of God (the Kingdom of God) can man be liberated from the mystery of the world, and thereby be freed to become fully autonomous in the world.

What should most excite our interest in this position is its conjunction of the radical transcendence of God with the full autonomy of man. Man was created in the image of God, and it is the destiny of man to be the agent and instrument of God in fulfilling God's purpose in the world. God is the absolutely sovereign and transcendent Creator, and man was created in His image as the fully autonomous creature. Moreover, it is through a pure and total faith in God the Creator that man fulfills the purpose of the creation by becoming sovereign over the world. There can be no question that this theological position incorporates an exceedingly important and rarely articulated historical truth. For it is only in the Christian world that God has been manifest as the radically transcendent God, only in Christendom that God has appeared in consciousness and experience as hidden and alien, as totally inaccessible, apart and beyond. While it was only in the course of a long historical movement that the Christian God became manifest as the alien and hidden God, we must take due note of the fact that this is a uniquely Christian phenomenon. So likewise it was only in Christendom or, more specifically, only in modern Western history that man appeared to himself as a unique and autonomous center of consciousness. Indeed, it was not until that period in Western history when God was fully manifest as being wholly isolated and apart that man discovered himself as an absolutely unique and autonomous being. What the secular school of contemporary theology calls a radical and eschatological faith came to its full historical expression in the Western world in the seventeenth and eighteenth centuries. Only here and nowhere else in history do we find the conjunction of God appearing to consciousness as apart and beyond, and self-consciousness appearing to itself as its own individual and unique creator.

Today each of us inherits, albeit in a crumbling and empty form, what was once manifest as a self-consciousness which is its own creator. Since it is only in the modern Western world that selfhood or self-consciousness has appeared as absolute, as its own autonomous and unique creator, it is incumbent upon us to examine the theological roots of this phenomenon. Is it not possible to maintain that there is an essential relationship between the image of God as the sovereign Creator and the image of man as the autonomous and sovereign ruler over the world? If, as many Christian theologians affirm, it is only Christianity which has truly known the sovereignty of God, does this apprehension underlie and stand behind the modern Western apprehension of the autonomy of selfhood? Is not the full autonomy of man a mirror or reflection of what faith once had known as the autonomy of God? Does not a self-consciousness which apprehends its own center or ego as the maker or creator of itself reflect a form of power which faith had long associated with the sovereignty of God? Is not the new and infinite mystery which the modern West discovered in the human person a mystery which had long appeared in the form of the transcendent mystery of God? Is not the modern sense of the unique individuality of the human person a reverse reflection of what Christendom had come to know as the total solitude of God? Above all, is it not necessary theologically to affirm that a unique and autonomous selfhood is truly the image of an absolutely transcendent God?

There can be no gainsaying the historical truth that it is only in the modern West that God and selfhood jointly appear to consciouness as being absolute in their own inherent identities. It is also of vital importance to note that modern thinking and imagination envision the death of God as incorporating the advent of a new and total chaos. The modern consciousness knew or experienced the death of God only by passing through the dissolution of its own center and ground. Therein consciousness became alienated and estranged from itself. No longer could consciousness or self-consciousness know itself as its own ground. Pure or total selfhood now becomes alien or other to itself. For the self-alienation of consciousness in the modern world is a reflection of the dissolution or submersion of a previous center of consciousness. It is that form of consciousness which knows itself as its own center and ground which here becomes alienated and estranged from itself. Thus our modern experience of the death of God is a reflection of the dissolution of a uniquely modern form of consciousness. At the very least, the death of God in the modern world is the end or dissolution of the absolute and transcendent ego. That form of consciousness which knows itself as sovereign and autonomous here passes through its own dissolution. From this perspective, the death of God is the collapse of an absolute form of consciousness or self-consciousness. It is the end of that totally autonomous selfhood which was the unique creation of modern Western history.

Who could fail to note that so many of the most astute critics of the modern proclamation of the death of God insist that the death of God is the end of humanity? Virtually the whole body of orthodox and conservative theology is united in its insistence that an acceptance of the death of God is a submission to the dehumanization of man. What they fail to point out is that it is not simply man but the autonomy and sovereignty of man which comes to an end with the modern historical realization of the death of God. It is that form of consciousness and selfhood which is enclosed within itself, or isolated and apart by virtue of its own autonomy, which collapses as a consequence of the advent of the death of God. The full historical actualization of the death of God brings an end to a unique and autonomous selfhood, an end to all forms of consciousness or self-consciousness which apprehend the ego or the self as its own autonomous and unique creator. The night brought on by the death of God is a night in which every individual identity perishes. When the heavens are darkened, and God disappears, man does not stand autonomous and alone. He ceases to stand. Or, rather, he ceases to stand *out* from the world and himself, ceases to be autonomous and apart. No longer can self-hood or self-consciousness stand purely and solely upon itself: no longer can a unique and individual identity stand autonomously upon itself. The death of the transcendence of God embodies the death of all autonomous selfhood, an end of all humanity which is created in the image of the absolutely sovereign and transcendent God.

This end can be named by a contemporary eschatological faith as the realization of an eternal death or Hell. Now the individual death of Jesus can be actualized in the dissolution of the center of self-consciousness. Thus a faith grounded in the final death of an individual selfhood, the eternal death of Jesus, can name the dissolution of all autonomous selfhood as the historical realization of the descent into Hell. The descent of Christ into Hell is only initially and originally an individual act or movement of descent. When the eternal death of Jesus is incorporated into the body of humanity, and incorporated by a form of faith revolving about a continual dying with Christ, then the original descent into Hell can gradually and progressively be actualized in the universal body of humanity. Then the individual and eternal death of Jesus is comprehensively and universally realized in the dissolution of the center or ground of all forms of autonomous and individual self-consciousness. For the actual and real dissolution or death of the center of consciousness brings about the end of all autonomous self-consciousness. Yet the dissolution of autonomous self-consciousness is simultaneously the end of all truly individual selfhood, the end of the autonomous ego or the self which is only itself.

Once the ground of an autonomous consciousness has been emptied or dissolved, then there can be no individual center of consciousness, or no center which is autonomous and unique. With the disappearance of the ground of individual selfhood, the unique "I" or personal ego progressively becomes a mere reflection or echo of its former self. Now the "I" takes into itself everything from which it had withdrawn itself, and therefore it ceases to stand apart. In losing its autonomy, it loses its own unique center or ground, and thereby it loses everything which had once appeared as an individual identity or "face." Facelessness and loss of identity now become the mark of everyone, as everyone becomes no one, and the "I" is inseparable from the "other." Individual selfhood does not simply or literally come to an end or disappear; it appears in the other. Only in the other does the individual appear or become real, for it is only in the eyes or the glance or the touch of the other that the individual becomes himself. We need not wonder that it is now possible objectively to record what a Kierkegaard, a Dostoyevsky, or a Nietzsche had prophetically foreseen as the destiny of our time. Nor should the Christian be surprised that the modern imagination has envisioned the disappearance of selfhood as a descent into Hell.

IV ✳

All the higher expressions of religion, by one means or another, envision salvation or release as an interior passage through the dissolution or reversal of the self. Nor is it simply any form of selfhood which is here dissolved or reversed: it is rather a given form of selfhood, that form of selfhood which is most naturally or inherently itself. Therefore a Christian dying with Christ is not unique insofar as it embodies a dying to self. As we previously observed, it is unique only inasmuch as it embodies a particular and individual death, the final or eternal death of Jesus. But a dying with and in the individual death of Jesus demands a dying of a particular and individual form of the self. It demands a dying of that form of the self which is most immediately and interiorly our own. Consequently, a Christian dying with Christ is not a dying of an eternal, an unchanging, or a universal form of selfhood. Nor is it a dying of simply any form of selfhood which happens to be present to us. Rather, it demands the death of that self which appears to be most real in our consciousness and experience, that individual "I" which we would claim as being most interiorly and autonomously our own.

In the Christian perspective, death assumes ever-varying meanings and identities, as each age or period or form of humanity creates its own individual images of death. Not only is each Christian called to die his own individual death, and to die it continually in Christ, but every individual time and place calls for its own particular form of death. In each case, a particular form of death calls for a death or dying of a particular and individual form of selfhood. For it is that form of selfhood which is most real in its own time and situation which must die to realize a Christian dying with Christ. What, then, can dying with Christ mean to us in our time and situation? If everything which we have known as selfhood is disappearing in our midst, then how can eternal death be authentic or real to us? If we have no fixed center, then how can dying to such a center be meaningful or real? How can we die our own death, our own individual death, if we cannot seize, or even call upon, a truly individual form of selfhood? If it is impossible to name the selfhood which is present to us, how can we envision or even speak of death?

Despite our apparent loss of identity, no age has spoken more eloquently of death than our own. It could even be said that no previous age has so forcefully envisioned the individuality and finality of death. What we have lost in the autonomy and uniqueness of selfhood, we would seem to have gained in our experience and understanding of death. Where self was, death now reigns; where an autonomous selfhood appeared as its own creator, death or nothingness now appears as both the source and goal of the self. In losing all sense of a fixed, or autonomous, or unchanging form of selfhood, have we not come to identify the presence or the presences of the self with a transient and ever-vanishing series of real moments in time? Once an absolute form of selfhood had vanished from our horizon, were we not given a new and overwhelming sense of the actuality and finality of concrete points of time and space? And a sense of a self or point within us which is most real when it is most distant from all which had previously appeared as self? Or from all which was once manifest as the autonomy, the sovereignty, and the purity of a selfhood which is its own source or creator?

No longer can selfhood appear in self-consciousness as a transcendent and autonomous center. Nor can it truly appear in the form of an isolated and unique identity. As opposed to what was once manifest as a unique and individual center of consciousness, selfhood has increasingly and ever more pervasively become anonymous. It has lost or is losing everything which sets it apart and within; as the mysterious interior depths of selfhood have been emptied into the immediacy of concrete points in time and space. So far from appearing as a self-enclosed and autonomous center of consciousness, that self which has become real to us is a naked point in time and space, a point released from a transcendent ground. That self which is most real to us is that self which has appeared and become real as a consequence of the dissolution of transcendence or the death of God. Selfhood can no longer appear as its own center and ground, or as its own maker or creator. We have lost an interior sense of the transcendence of the ego or the self, and in losing that sense we have lost the autonomy of the self. Who is there among us who can truly know or identify himself with a unique and autonomous selfhood, a selfhood standing fully within and apart?

One way into the meaning of that new selfhood which has become actual and manifest in our midst is by conceiving it as a negation or reversal of that transcendence which stands apart and beyond. The new selfhood into which we are being initiated is neither isolated nor apart. So far from being an autonomous center, it is unenclosed and unconfined. Indeed, it is not truly a center at all. Or, at least, it is not a fixed center, or a center deriving its identity from a unique and eternal self. What we have most deeply lost is all sense of the perpetuity or eternity of selfhood, all sense of a self standing outside of the contingencies and vicissitudes of time. Therefore we have lost all awareness of our transcendent identity, and can no longer identify ourselves as standing outside the horizons of time and space. With this loss of a transcendent identity, we have also lost all real sense of the interior distance of selfhood, whether that distance be conceived as deriving from the self's ground in a transcendent beyond or a transcendent within. No longer do we have an awareness of infinite heights or of infinite depths, unless those heights and depths are conceived and envisioned as lying *within* what we have come to know as the infinite boundaries of space and time.

To reach the selfhood or identity which is now being given us, we must turn away from every previous identity of the self. Above all we must resist and oppose every nostalgic and backward-looking call to return to what once was manifest as either the autonomy or eternity of selfhood. So likewise must we resist and oppose all nostalgic yearning for the unique individuality of selfhood. Here, the Christian has been given new images of death as well as new ways to the actualization of eternal death.

Now the Christian is called to name the autonomy and eternity of selfhood as images of death, and as images of deaths which we must die. It is precisely by negating our yearning for autonomy and transcendence that we can die the eternal death which is now given us. Not only must we negate all such yearning, we must also reverse it. Or, more truly stated, the negation of selfhood to which we are called is a reversal of everything which is manifest as the autonomy and eternity of the self. But this can only mean that we are called to die the death of God, the death of the God who has been manifest to us as absolute sovereignty and pure transcendence. Only in the modern world has eternal death become manifest to consciousness as the death of God. Yet the eternal death which the Christian knows has its source and ground in the death of Jesus. Thus the Christian can now die the death of God as the actualization for us and in us of the original and eternal death of Jesus.

By recognizing that pure transcendence is the ground of a totally autonomous selfhood, we can also recognize that the way to the abolition or reversal of the autonomy of selfhood is by interiorly passing through a dissolution of transcendence. Such an actual and interior passage can never be effected by an immersion in the public and objective realm of anonymity. It must rather be accomplished by an individual act of dying. And not only a dying to our public image or our persona, but more deeply a dying to that private selfhood which is most interiorly and individually our own. Interiorly, we seize upon our autonomy and our transcendence as our deepest identity. Or, rather, we imagine that our apparent autonomy and our apparent transcendence are our truest identity. But this is an appearance which has become manifest as an illusion in our time. For everything which was once manifest as the autonomy and transcendence of selfhood is dissolving in our midst, and dissolving in such a manner that its emptiness is now implicitly or explicitly spoken and lived by all. Cannot the Christian freely pass through this dissolution of transcendence and autonomy as an actualization for us and in us of the eternal death of Jesus and the descent of Christ into Hell?

If we can but name our darkness, not only can we freely pass within it, but we can know our darkness as our own. As opposed to every Stoic call to submit passively to our destiny as our fate, an eschatological faith calls upon us to accept our end as our beginning—not a beginning which is a primordial and original beginning, but rather a beginning which is the advent of a new or apocalyptic age. By knowing that our darkness and emptiness are reflections or images of the dissolution of the transcendence and sovereignty of God, we can be open to the death or end of a divine transcendence and sovereignty as the way to our eternal death. The Christian is liberated from every God but the God who is present and real in Christ. If the only Christ whom faith can know is the Christ who is present in Hell or eternal death, then the only God who here and now can be known by faith is the God who is manifest as eternal death. Not only is God manifest to us as eternal death, but He is actual and real within us in the form of eternal death. If we can know the dissolution of sovereignty and transcendence as the death of God for us, then we can pass through the death or reversal of an autonomous and transcendent selfhood as the way to a new and more comprehensive presence and identity of Christ.

V ✳

From the perspective of our own time, the eschatological call of Jesus initially appears as a nihilistic call to madness or to death. Certainly the Kingdom of God whose dawning he announces would appear to be the absolute antithesis of everything which is manifest to us as world and reality. It is just for this reason that the way which he embodied and taught has been judged again and again in our century to be totally irrelevant and meaningless to us. What human meaning can an eschatological way have in a time and world which have lost all sense of the reality or the presence of the transcendent and the beyond? Must not the way of Jesus be for us an empty and nostalgic call to a time and identity which is wholly and irreversibly past? Does not an acceptance of that new future before us demand a repudiation of every way and call from the past? How can the ancient name of Christ be anything for us but a way to a resistance and refusal of that new human identity which has dawned so awesomely and so overwhelmingly in our world?

Once the name of Christ is identified with the Christ of Christian orthodoxy, it is clear beyond doubt that the new humanity which has become manifest in our time is a form of humanity which has negated and reversed the name of Christ. As opposed to the orthodox image of the eternal and transcendent Christ, modern man has passed through a dissolution or disintegration of transcendence, thereby losing all awareness of the reality of a transcendent eternity. With the collapse of a transcendent eternity, the ancient name of Christ has clearly become invisible and unreal in the modern world. So likewise the name of Jesus would seem to have become empty for us. Or, at least, every meaning and identity of Jesus have become empty and unreal which are integrally or essentially related to the orthodox image of the transcendent Christ who is the Word or Son of God. Yet a radical Christian faith has long called for a negation and reversal of the transcendent and eternal Christ as the way to that Christ who is totally here and now for us. It is the radical claim that once faith itself has truly reversed the transcendent Christ, then Christ himself will appear and be real to us, and his new presence will actualize an apocalyptic Kingdom in our midst.

Apocalyptic visions are commonly judged to be pathological and unreal because they are seen as being the consequence of a loss of relationship with reality. Accordingly, an apocalyptic future is considered unreal because it is the product of either a flight from or a rebellion against the reality of the world. At most, apocalyptic visions are ordinarily seen as the result of historical periods of crisis and transition. It is the breakdown of an historical tradition or a social class or group which generates apocalyptic visions, and the only reality such visions contain is a record of the interior vacuity and terror of their seers. No doubt ours is a time of intense apocalyptic vision, but it is also a time of radical historical transition. Who can doubt that apocalypticism is a pathological fantasy and delusion brought on by the collapse of the human and social identity of those who create and embrace it? But if an apocalyptic future is an illusion, does an apocalyptic judgment and condemnation embody an illusion of the same kind? Is the no-saying of an apocalyptic and prophetic judgment just as illusory and pathological as the yes-saying of an apocalyptic hope? Is an apocalyptic assault upon the given or apparent reality of the world simply the result of a pathological loss of contact with reality?

These questions may in part be confronted by taking up the question of the ethical meaning of an apocalyptic way of faith, particularly insofar as such a meaning may be manifest in our time. Before we can become open to the meaning of an apocalyptic or fully eschatological ethical way, however, we must realize that it is wholly removed from the dominant systems of Western ethics. Previously we observed that a fully eschatological way transcends the normative or imperative form of Western ethics, and this because an eschatological and apocalyptic way already embodies the goal to which it points. A

purely eschatological way also transcends or stands outside of Western ethics inasmuch as it is free of an essential ground in the civilization and the social institutions of
Western history. As Herbert Marcuse has so persuasively
pointed out, all of the ethical systems of Western philoso-
phy presuppose that history or civilization has finally established the institutions and relationships within whose
framework man can realize and fulfill himself. Freedom,
or goodness, or happiness is always realized for Western
ethics within the framework and structure of an already
established social and cultural world. Man's nature is
given and immobile, and so likewise are his ends or his
goals. Ethics is a way of moving toward or realizing those
goals through the given conditions of our actual situation
in the world. Yet an eschatological way not only challenges but envisions the end of all such conditions and re-
joices in the presence of a radically new humanity.
Therefore a truly apocalyptic way will embody little or
nothing of what has been manifest as ethics in Christendom.

We can see at once that there is nothing comparable in
Western ethics to an eschatological judgment and condemnation. True, we find the full equivalent of such a
judgment in the radical expressions of modern Western
thought, as witness Kierkegaard, Marx, Nietzsche, and
Freud. But all of these thinkers were forced to oppose
and transcend the established principles of ethics, and it
is significant that Hegel was able to construct a system of
ethics only by largely abandoning his dialectical system.

It is also significant that when these radical expressions of Western thinking have been socially and culturally institutionalized, they cease to be radical. Doubtless this is the inevitable fate of a prophetic movement when it is incorporated into a priestly form and body; but it should increase our awareness that an eschatological way will invariably be in radical tension with all ecclesiastical and social authority. For the hope of an apocalyptic way can be realized only by passing through the full movement of an eschatological judgment.

We can see the essential relationship between an apocalyptic affirmation and an eschatological judgment by noting the integral relationship between the new humanity which is dawning in our midst and the dissolution or disintegration of that form of humanity which was once dominant in our history. If a full or real selfhood was previously manifest as being grounded in an autonomous and transcendent center of consciousness, now we are being called to a new form of humanity which is losing every genuine sign of autonomy and transcendence. That seemingly infinite distance separating every center of consciousness is now collapsing, and with it is collapsing everything which once gave the self the appearance of transcendence and autonomy. No longer can individual selfhood appear as autonomous and unique, nor can individual groups and bodies apprehend themselves as being truly particular and distinct. A new consciousness is becoming actual about and within us which promises to dissolve every former human and social identity. Contempo-

rary apocalyptic vision can celebrate this new consciousness as an historical realization of the new creation. But to do so it must will the death within us of everything which is bound to the old humanity of our past.

Can an apocalyptic faith name this new consciousness
as the contemporary appearance and reality of Christ?
Can it respond to the new world and the new humanity
of our future as an embodiment of the eschatological way
and identity of Jesus? Can it embrace the darkness and
emptiness of our world as the fruits of an eschatological
judgment and salvation? More concretely stated, can the
contemporary Christian accept the loss of interior distance and autonomy as a realization of the call of Jesus?
Is the Kingdom working in *our* midst, in the midst of our
interior collapse and disintegration? Can we know the
death of our interior autonomy and transcendence as a
descent into the realm and the identity of the other? Of
all others? Does otherness itself collapse and disappear
with the full realization of an interior death? Can we celebrate the dissolution of our unique and particular ego as
the initial appearance of a universal humanity? All of
these questions drive us to the ethical meaning of a contemporary apocalyptic way of faith. For each of them impels us to an eschatological judgment upon everything
within ourselves which craves an autonomous and transcendent identity. And each of them points the way to an
apocalyptic future when eternal death will have been
finally realized and fulfilled, and Christ will be all in all.

Yet a grave danger lies here before us, a danger which

has ever threatened apocalyptic faith, and one which is as powerful now as ever. This is the terrible temptation for faith of withdrawing into a false and private interior, an interior isolated from the actual world of the other, and free of the actuality of the exterior world. So grave has this danger become that there would seem to be no human way of distinguishing faith from fantasy or vision from delusion. Not only has an ancient way of faith become empty and unreal, but it is increasingly true that faith can no longer function in the established ethical realm of personal decision and individual action. What can personal decision and individual action mean to us? What will they mean to us? Must faith live or die with the continued presence of the individual who can act individually and who can make personal and individual decisions? These questions have long been driving faith to the wall, and they do more than a little to explain the deeply reactionary political choices which were made by almost all of the great modern revolutionary religious thinkers. For if faith must be grounded in personal decision and individual action, then it would seem to be closed to that real future which now lies before us. Must we not finally confess that faith now faces the inescapable demand of embracing the historical actuality of our consciousness and experience as the sole presence and identity of a total and eschatological Christ?

This is the decision the Christian is now called upon to make. Just as in ancient apocalyptic faith, an individual decision can here have no effect upon an eschatological realization. Indeed, it is only insofar as an individual decision is a universal decision that it can be realized eschatologically. It is only the new Adam, or the new creation, or the new humanity, which can fully and truly embody and realize an eschatological act or decision. So, ethically *and* eschatologically considered, it is the private and purely individual act which now must be judged to be guilty. Sin is a private and isolated state of autonomous existence. And the forgiveness of sin is the dissolution and reversal of that existence, the abolition and transcendence of the private ego. Sin is isolation from the actuality of the other, and the forgiveness of sin is the disintegration of all that interior distance separating men from men and self from self. Sin is a false and illusory inwardness or outwardness, isolating the interior from the exterior, and wholly divorcing the immediacy of the inner world from the actuality of the outer world. And the forgiveness of sin is a new creation in which the inner and outer realms are united, and the interior depths of inwardness are identical with the exterior and outer depths of every other. The forgiveness of sin is the New Jerusalem, the apocalyptic name of love, and the contemporary name of Christ.

5

The
New
Jerusalem

*

I ✳

If apocalyptic vision has been reborn in the modern world, its rebirth is inseparable from the collapse and disintegration of an established way of faith. Just as ancient apocalypticism was born in the exilic and postexilic periods of Israel's history, when the world of ancient Israel had already come to an end, so likewise modern apocalypticism has evolved out of the death or end of Christendom. Modern apocalypticism has itself negated and reversed the world of faith out of which it has arisen, and thus a new apocalyptic vision is a primary ground of a seemingly post-Christian history. Indeed, this new vision is so estranged from its biblical source that thus far it has not been possible fully to identify it. Yet there can be little doubt that apocalyptic vision abounds in the modern world, as witness imaginative seers as diverse as Blake, Rilke, Kafka, Joyce, and Beckett. At the very least we have been given fragments of genuine apocalyptic vision, and the vast distance of these fragments

173

from their New Testament counterparts should give us some sense of the revolution in theological thinking which our actual situation now demands. Already one cardinal principle clearly stands before us: there is no way into this new vision apart from a negation and transcendence of all of our inherited and established modes of theological thinking and analysis.

Not only has the great body of theological thinking been closed to that new and radical vision which has dawned in the modern world, but that vision itself defies all analysis employing the established theological categories of Christianity. So much is this the case that innumerable interpreters have been driven to Hindu and Buddhist categories in their attempt to understand the world of modern Western vision. At the same time there is not a single major artist or thinker in the modern world who can definitively be judged to be Christian. Who can any longer say what either faith or vision now mean to the Christian? While lacking all assurance or certainty as to the meaning of vision in our world, we must never lose sight of the necessity of seeking the meaning of vision, even if such a quest results again and again in failure and defeat. From a theological point of view, it is vitally important to open ourselves to a wholly new meaning of faith and vision, with the expectation that a contemporary Christian vision will be worlds apart from its historical predecessors. First, we must disabuse ourselves of the priestly and ecclesiastical conviction that Christianity has already fully and finally revealed or unveiled itself. For in our turbulent and chaotic situation everything which we have been given as faith is tumbling in our midst, and we must either consign Christianity to a lost and increasingly forgotten past, or be prepared to accept the advent of a new Christianity which thus far has been theologically unrecognizable and unnamable.

At the very time when all established Christian forms and categories have fallen into eclipse, whole new religious worlds have dawned about us, and these worlds appear with the greatest power when they are most alien to the Christian world which we have lost. Obviously this is true of the world or worlds of Oriental vision, and it surely cannot be accidental that these worlds were discovered and initially explored by the West in the same period when modern seers were announcing the end of Christendom and the death of God. Who can doubt that the loss of God was an essential ground for the modern Western understanding of the Orient? For not only does the East know little or nothing of what the West has known as God, but the fullness of vision in the East precludes the possibility of the apprehension of deity. Or, at least, it negates every form of deity which stands isolated and enclosed within itself. Even Western words for faith and religion have been barriers to an understanding of the East, for here we have been initiated into a world of total vision which allows for no separation or division between a realm of the here and the now and the realm of the apart and the beyond. Simply to be open to Oriental vision is to be freed from the givenness and finality of Oc-

cidental religious forms and categories. What can faith as
we have known it mean when vision has finally dissolved
the distance and the otherness of the transcendent and
the sacred?

What we have been given in the West as the religious
and theological category of transcendence assumes a new
meaning when seen from an Oriental perspective. The
transcendence which we have known is identical with the
primordial nature and identity of God. Furthermore, it is
by knowing the world as the creation and God as the
Creator that we have known transcendence as an impassable and infinite distance between the world and God.
Already we have observed that it is precisely such an understanding of transcendence which has precluded the
possibility of a full and Christian understanding of the
Kingdom of God. For inasmuch as the transcendence of
God is an eternal and unbridgeable gulf between God
and the world, there can be no possibility of the advent
or actualization of a Kingdom of God which will draw all
things into itself. But in the perspective of the Oriental
vision we can come to understand that what we have
known as the transcendence of God is a reflection of a
particular situation: the condition of fallen man confronting the realm of the sacred and the beyond from which
he as a fallen creature is alienated and estranged. We
need not doubt that this is our actual condition, and that
it has been only in a condition of fallenness that we have
known and experienced faith. But neither can the Christian doubt that in Christ we have been offered or given a

redemption from fallenness, and that a Kingdom of God is present in Christ which transforms and transcends the fallen condition of man and the world.

Inevitably, we ourselves will remain estranged from Christ and the Kingdom so long as we remain bound to what we have known as the transcendence of God. Moreover, we will remain bound to a divine transcendence so long as we understand transcendence as the eternal and primordial nature of God. Yet the Oriental vision can release us from such an understanding. For it confronts us with a vision of an original and primordial Totality which lies beyond what we have understood as the primordial nature of God. In the perspective of this vision, we can see that the West has never known a truly or fully primordial reality, has never known, at least in its Christian traditions, a primordial reality which is the original face or form of all reality whatsoever. Thus far it would seem that the Christian vision is necessarily a fallen vision: a vision apprehending both God and the world from the perspective of the Fall. It is what Christianity apprehends as the finality of the Fall which makes impossible for the Christian a full vision of an original innocence, just as it likewise closes the Christian to the possibility of a full and total vision of God. If nothing else, the Orient can teach us that Christianity has never embodied a total vision, and thus the Christian has never truly or fully known God as a Totality or an All.

Of course, Christianity has been given visions of the All, as witness not only its apocalyptic and mystical visions, but also its imaginative visions as embodied in a Dante, a Milton, or a Blake. But Christianity has never envisioned God as the All, for it has been unable to dissociate the name of God from a divine transcendence dividing the creature from the Creator. Consequently, Christianity has been unable to envision or conceive a primordial Totality, an original All comprehending every form of reality. It is just such a primordial Totality or original All which lies at the center of Oriental vision. So it is that the Oriental vision presents us with another way to the meaning of an eschatological faith and vision. If eschatological vision is directed to the final End, to the New Jerusalem, then this End can never be meaningful apart from its relationship to the primordial Beginning. Insofar as Christianity has known God as the transcendent Creator, it has been closed to a primordial Beginning, to the initial or original form and identity of the All. But it is just because Christianity has been closed to a primordial Beginning that virtually all of its forms have been unable to envision an eschatological All. Not until an original Totality or Beginning comes within the purview of eschatological faith and vision can that vision know the New Jerusalem as an apocalyptic or eschatological All.

It is precisely by taking the Oriental vision with utmost seriousness that Christian theological thinking can be given a new way into the meaning and reality of its eschatological ground. While there is no possibility of reversing history and returning to the original and primitive form of the Christian faith, there is nevertheless a genuine possibility of a new form of faith revolving about a *new* epiphany of the New Jerusalem. If the symbolic names of Brahman-Atman, Nirvana, Sunyata, and Tao can be understood by the Christian thinker as images of the initial or original form of the All, then he can be given a way to an understanding of the New Jerusalem as an apocalyptic image of the final actualization and realization of the All. Then we could understand that the primordial reality is not to be identified with the primordial nature of God, but rather with the primordial form and identity of the All. So likewise by this means we can be freed from the otherwise all too alluring temptation of thinking that the Kingdom of God is the consequent nature and identity of God, as though it were only in God that the world and humanity can finally be actual and real. Once the Oriental vision is absorbed into Christian thinking, then the new aeon or new creation need not be understood as the final or consequent form of God or the world, but rather as the final and ultimate expression and realization of all reality. Accordingly, a final or eschatological realization of reality could then be understood as abolishing all polarities and divisions, including the polarity between God and the world, and the division between humanity and deity.

This path also opens the way to a new and comprehensive understanding of the Fall. So long as the movement and reality of the Fall is confined and limited to its effect upon man and the world, as it is in Christian orthodoxy, then redemption can only be envisioned as a transformation of man and the world. The advent and dawning of the Kingdom of God must then be understood as a new openness of humanity to the eternal nature and glory of God. The dawning of the Kingdom of God is then conceived as the birth in human consciousness of an awareness of the unchanging identity and reality of God. Here, nothing occurs in the advent of either Christ or the Kingdom of God to affect the fundamental or underlying nature of reality. But if the Fall is conceived in a total and comprehensive sense, then it must be conceived as affecting God Himself. From this point of view, everything which fallen man envisions and conceives as God is a fallen form of God. The mystery, the distance, the majesty, and the transcendence of God can here be understood as products of the Fall. This is not to say that such forms of God are simple products of human projection and illusion. On the contrary, it is to take the fallen condition of man with ultimate seriousness, and to affirm that fallen man truly encounters and knows a fallen form of deity. Sin is not an illusory state, nor is original sin a product of fantasy and delusion: to affirm that the Fall effected a transformation of reality is to affirm that the horror embedded at the center of man and the world is actually horror. Only by naming our darkness as the consequence of the Fall can we know that our darkness is truly darkness. Otherwise we must relapse into a state of passivity in the presence of evil, thereby sanctioning evil itself by identifying it as humanly meaningless or given and natural.

There is no possibility of taking sin and the Fall with total seriousness so long as God is understood to be unaffected by the Fall. If the transcendent God is the Christian name of the source and the ground of existence, then the Christian can recognize that the world is truly fallen only by acknowledging the fallen identity of the transcendent God. Therein the Christian can understand that the divine transcendence is a consequence of an original fall from the primordial Totality. A divine transcendence is inseparable from its ground in an alienation and estrangement of man from God and man from man. Simply to affirm the impassable distance of God or the sacred realm is to sanction the brokenness of existence by accepting the eternal nature of an alienated world. When God is envisioned as being eternally transcendent and apart, then the quest for total redemption is judged to be sinful and illusory, and man and the world are radically subordinated to God. Then only God can be fully real, only God can be the subject of ultimate concern, and only God can be the object of total attention and devotion. What could more decisively signify the fallen state of man than an ultimate faith in the transcendence of God? On the other hand, if the fallen condition of man is truly actual and real, then the transcendence of God is likewise real, and the transcendent God will be present wherever man truly exists in a state of brokenness and alienation. Apart from the presence of God Himself, fallen man exists in a nameless condition, finally being unable even to name darkness itself as night.

Yet to affirm that the transcendence of God is real in a fallen and alienated world is not to affirm that the transcendence of God is unchanging and eternal. The mere fact that divine transcendence in the Christian and Western sense is unknown in the Orient witnesses to the particular and not the universal nature of the Christian vision of God. This is not to say that the Christian vision of God is not essential to apocalyptic vision. Nor is it to say that the full or pure transcendence of God is an ultimate barrier to full redemption. On the contrary, it is to identify what the Christian has known as the transcendence of God as an essential ground of what the Christian has been given as apocalyptic vision and full redemption. If apocalyptic vision is only fully present in Christianity, then we must recognize that the Christian proclamation of the dawning and triumph of the Kingdom of God is a proclamation reflecting the movement and transformation of what the Christian knows as God. It is God Himself who dawns in the Kingdom, it is the transcendence of God which is here actualized as total immanence. The advent of Christ and the Kingdom of God embody a transformation of the center of reality. In negating and reversing the transcendence of God, Christ and the Kingdom embody a negation and reversal of the fallenness of God. But the Fall is not reversed in the sense that man is returned to an original harmony and communion with

the transcendent Creator. It is rather that the transcendence of God is negated to make possible an eschatological
consummation of a broken and alienated Totality.

II ✳

When an original Totality or All is envisioned as the
primordial ground of the Kingdom of God or the New Jerusalem, then the New Jerusalem can be envisioned as
the final or eschatological realization of an original or primordial Totality. Such a mode of total vision also brings
with it a new and more comprehensive understanding of
the Fall. Now the Fall can be envisioned as a fall of an
original Totality or All: it is the center or primordial
ground of reality which becomes darkened and broken by
the Fall. As a consequence of the movement and actuality
of the Fall, alienation and estrangement penetrate the
center of reality, as the primordial Totality becomes divided and alienated from itself. Nothing whatsoever
stands apart from the "descending" and chaotic movement of the Fall, as every individual entity now stands
out in a new solitude and isolation. For with the loss of
an original unity, harmony, or coherence, distance arises
and creates every new center of experience, thus bringing
about a new and solitary selfhood which is its own individual center or ground. From a radical Christian
perspective, we could say that God Himself is the primary embodiment of a solitary and isolated selfhood.
Then it would be possible to say that the divine tran-

scendence is the source and ground of a comprehensive transcendence, a fallen transcendence isolating and dividing every center of consciousness and experience. The pure or radical transcendence of God—a transcendence which has been historically present only in Christian faith and vision—could then be identified as the primary consequence of the Fall, a consequence which is itself the ground of a fallen history and experience.

By this means it would be possible not only to bring together but also to integrally relate two of the most distinctive if not unique affirmations of Christianity: the radical transcendence of God and the finality of the Fall. One of the most important and significant universals in the history of religions is the image of an original or primordial paradise and bliss. We find this image almost everywhere in the world's mythology, but, significantly enough, a pure or full image of paradise has never been present in Christianity. Or, rather, when it has been present, as in the Book of Revelation, or Dante, or Blake, it has always been a vision of a future, a final, or an eschatological paradise, and never a vision of an original or primordial bliss. For a full or total image of a primordial bliss is necessarily an image of an *original* Totality, and when the transcendence of God is present in faith and vision there can be no vision of an *original* All. There can be no awareness of an original *Totality* of bliss so long as the transcendence of God is known as being eternal and immutable, and is unknown or invisible as a fallen and alienated transcendence. The Christian is banished from

the original garden of Eden, and banished by his knowledge of the Fall. So it is that Christianity alone among
the religions of the world has known the full reality and
finality of the Fall. The Christian has no way of returning
to an original Totality, for with the advent in consciousness and experience of what the Christian knows as the
Fall, an original Totality disintegrates and "disappears."

All too naturally we find the conjunction in Oriental vision of an absence of awareness of a divine transcendence
with a full awareness of an original and total bliss. Wherever we turn in the higher expressions of Oriental religion, whether to Taoism, Hinduism, Buddhism, Jainism,
or Sankhya-Yoga, we find religious and mystical ways to
an original Totality. Not only does a full and total image
of an original Totality dominate the mystical ways of the
East, but these ways are themselves concrete paths to an
original and undifferentiated consciousness. Nothing
comparable to these Eastern ways of totally reversing all
present and actual states of consciousness and experience
is present in the West, for Western religious ways, with
the possible exception of the Kabbalah, have no way back
to an original All. From a Western point of view, one of
the most alien and exotic symbols of the East is that primary Eastern symbol of total calm or quiescence, a calm
in which all movement and motion disappears, and in
which all individual identities either pass into each other
or exist in such a state of mutual harmony that no individual identity is "other" to another. Here, the river of
time ceases to flow; or, if it flows, it flows in a continuum

abolishing every distinction between present, future, and past. Everything which the West has known as process, movement, and energy is absent from this vision of quiescence. Therefore, to Western eyes, this vision is totally unreal. But it is unreal to us only insofar as we are unable to detach ourselves from active selfhood and conscious movement. It is our very bondage to an actual and present state of consciousness and experience which closes us to a vision of total calm. Accordingly, from an Eastern point of view, it is the activity and temporality of the Western consciousness which bars its return to or realization of an original quiescence.

In Christian terms, we could say that it is the fallenness of consciousness which makes impossible for consciousness and experience the realization of a total and undifferentiated quiescence. But it is just this fallenness which makes possible the full apprehension and experience of movement and process. Apart from a fully active state of consciousness, there would be nothing present of what the West has known as time and motion. So it is that a Christian could say that it is the fallenness of consciousness which creates or makes possible everything which we have known as reality and world. It is the actuality of the Fall which effects a standing out of consciousness, an activity of consciousness in which consciousness stands upon or expresses itself in an individual and active center. Movement and activity now lie at the center of consciousness, and it is this action or actuality which must be judged to be a consequence of the Fall. The Christian can speak all too spontaneously of the universality of the Fall: for the West, unlike the East, has evolved a form of consciousness wherein total affirmation and activity are the arena of consciousness, and a consciousness which is not grounded in an active and individual will to be is not recognized as consciousness at all.

When the Christian takes the Oriental vision with full seriousness, he can see that Eastern vision embodies the original form of the active and individual consciousness which he knows. That we have lost or "forgotten" this original and undifferentiated consciousness we need have little doubt. But that does not make it unreal or illusory; it only makes it unreal to us. True, the Christian is alienated from the primordial bliss of an undifferentiated consciousness, and alienated precisely because he has fallen into the actuality and activity of an isolated and differentiated consciousness. As opposed to what the East has known as dreamless sleep or absolute inactivity and calm, the Christian is "awake." Yet the Fall is the source of our awakening, just as it is the ground of what appears to us as the brute reality of time and the world. Nevertheless, the Christian has long proclaimed that the Fall is a fortunate fall, a fall apart from which there can be neither real redemption nor an actual apocalypse. If an alienated and differentiated consciousness is a product of the Fall, it is nonetheless true that only such a consciousness can know and experience the actuality of time and movement. And the actuality of historical time and cosmic movement is an essential ground of the apocalypse, of a total transformation of the world and time.

Unlike those Eastern visions which parallel apocalyptic vision, apocalyptic vision does not proceed out of the dissolution or inactivity of an isolated and individual consciousness. On the contrary, it proceeds out of the transformation and movement of a consciousness existing in the actuality of time. Whereas Eastern vision knows temporal activity and actual movement as illusory and unreal, apocalyptic vision apprehends an actual historical and cosmic movement, an actual transformation of the center or ground of reality. There is no possibility here of the apprehension of an unchanging and original Totality, for an eschatological Kingdom or All is a new and final Totality. Only the dissolution or loss of an original Totality can make possible the advent and actualization of a final End. To the extent that the recollection or memory of an original Totality remains present in consciousness, that consciousness will be closed to the advent of the apocalypse, to the coming of a truly new Totality. Therefore the loss of a primordial All is a necessary presupposition for the appearance of an eschatological All, and the dissolution in consciousness of an original Totality is an essential ground for the actualization in consciousness of the New Jerusalem or the eschatological Christ. In this perspective, we could say that the advent of the Fall is the initial expression of the advent of the apocalypse. Or, otherwise stated, the advent of the Fall is the initial actualization of the eschatological Christ, of the Christ who embodies a descent into Hell.

We must return to the conjunction in Christian faith and vision of the finality of the Fall and the pure or radical transcendence of God. Once the transcendence of God is apprehended as a consequence of the Fall, as a product of the disintegration or dissolution of an original Totality, then a pure or radical transcendence can be linked with an isolated and differentiated consciousness. It could even be said that the more fallen and divided the state of consciousness, the more God will appear in a purely transcendent form. Christianity is par excellence the religion for fallen man because no other form of faith or vision embodies such an alien or "other" manifestation of deity or the sacred. Only Christianity knows the radical transcendence of God because only Christianity knows the finality of the Fall. It is the finality of the Fall which totally banishes the Christian from the immediate presence of the sacred, just as it is the reality of fallenness which seals the chasm between man and God and God and man. Here, there can be no genuine nostalgia for a primordial paradise, if only because that paradise has been hidden from view, and now can appear only in a dark and empty form. In confronting the pure transcendence of God, the Christian can know the sacred only as the Wholly Other, and thus the Christian can have no sense of the presence or actuality of the sacred. Accordingly, we might say that it is the disintegration and dissolution of the actuality of the sacred which effects or embodies the actuality of consciousness and time. We might also say that it is the advent of the pure or radical transcendence of God which totally releases consciousness from the primordial sacred, thereby allowing consciousness to be realized in the *actuality* of the world or the profane.

Once granting that Christianity embodies a moving or evolving form of faith and vision, then we could also say that the historical movement and development of Christianity reflects a progressive and ever more actual epiphany of the pure or radical transcendence of God. As God becomes ever more distant and alien to a Western form of consciousness, that consciousness itself progressively loses all sense of the reality of the sacred, and the total transcendence of God and the total disappearance of the sacred come to stand together in the modern consciousness. Consequently, we could say that it is the negation of the primordial sacred which makes possible the epiphany of the pure transcendence of God. When an original sacred has wholly disappeared from view, then God is manifest not only as the Wholly Other, but also as the alien and empty God whose presence empties and alienates everything which it touches. This is that totally transcendent manifestation of God which Blake envisioned as Satan and Melville as Moby Dick, which Hegel conceived as abstract Spirit and Nietzsche named as the deification of nothingness. Yet this is also that form of God whose very alien transcendence makes possible His dissolution and disintegration in consciousness. For only the totally alien and empty God can die in consciousness and experience. Only the empty and alien transcendence of God can be manifest by way of the image of the death of God Himself.

If we can come to understand that what the modern consciousness has known as the death of God is a consequence of the total negation of the primordial sacred—the consequence of what Mircea Eliade has called the Second Fall—then we can understand that an actual dissolution of an original Totality is an essential ground of modern vision. Paradoxically, or perhaps not so paradoxically, the death of God in the modern world has ushered in a whole new vision of a Totality or an All. Can we surmise that it is the final and total dissolution of an original Totality which opens consciousness and experience to an eschatological All? In any case, the fact remains that a Totality or All has once again become manifest to consciousness, and we are faced with the problem of the relation between an original and a final Totality. If a new and modern vision is apocalyptic, that is to say if it embodies a vision of an eschatological Totality or All, can we say that its vision is released by the final or ultimate death in consciousness and experience of every fragment or memory of an original Totality? By this means we could understand the death of God as the final negation of the primordial All, and therein once again come to understand that the death of God is an essential presupposition for the actualization of the New Jerusalem. For if the historical actualization of the death of God embodies a final negation and reversal of the primordial sacred, this very negation makes possible the actual and radical transformation of an original into a final Totality. Thus we could say that it is the original Totality which is actualized and realized eschatologically as the New Jerusalem. Nirvana is not "other" than Kingdom of God, just as Buddha is not "other" than Christ: Nirvana is the primordial ground of Kingdom of God, just as the New Jerusalem is the eschatological realization of Nirvana.

III ✳

The symbolic name of the Buddha (the name means Enlightened One) has fascinated the modern West as has no other mythical name from an exotic and seemingly alien world. This fascination is easily understandable on the part of the modern Christian world, a world in radical transition and transformation. For Buddhism and Christianity share at least three significant motifs. First, each has been a universal expression of religion, entering diverse cultural and historical worlds, and evolving new and more comprehensive forms in response to these worlds. Second, Buddhism and Christianity are the only religions in the world which have elevated the names, the images, or the identities of their founders to a supreme and absolute religious status. Finally, Buddhism and Christianity have made more total or absolute claims for love or compassion than have any other religions, and each has identified the compassion which it has celebrated and embodied as the "energy" or "body" of its founder. But while Orientals have commonly had little difficulty in identifying Christ as a form or avatar of the sacred reality which they know, Christians have thus far never been able to identify the Buddha as a face or form of Christ. Must we then conclude that a positive Western response to the name and claim of the Buddha must necessarily lead to an apostasy from the claim and name of Christ?

If the name of Christ is indissolubly associated for the Christian with the apocalyptic name of the Kingdom of God, then the name of the Buddha is likewise associated with the goal of Nirvana. On the one hand, Nirvana is one of a number of Oriental names and images for a total and primordial bliss. Yet, on the other hand, Nirvana is unique among Oriental images of bliss inasmuch as it is associated with a radical and totally negative way. Nirvana is a bliss that is absolutely beyond any experience or consciousness in which desire or craving (*tanha*) is present, for Nirvana is the "blowing out" of desire, a final victory over pain and illusion. As the ultimate goal of the Buddhist quest, Nirvana can be achieved only when everything that is unreal (i.e., everything that is painful and transitory) within consciousness and experience has been uprooted and destroyed. It demands the final cessation and dissolution of all forms and expressions of a personal and individual consciousness, just as it demands the total dissolution of all will and all desire. The Buddha is known by the Buddhist as being in a state of Nirvana;

hence he is not individually or personally present to the Buddhist. Nevertheless, the reality of the Buddha is present to the Buddhist. So likewise Nirvana is real even though it means the annihilation or extinction of everything which is present as "life" or "self." Indeed, the reality of Nirvana demands the annihilation of all other reality whatsoever.

A fully or totally negative way was reached by Buddhism only in its later or Mahayana expressions. Perhaps the deepest foundation of Mahayana Buddhism is the interior and intuitive experience of the ultimate identity of all reality. Not only does Mahayana Buddhism affirm that all sentient creatures are destined for salvation or release, but it also affirms that in the highest perspective all things even now are the Buddha-reality, or *tatha-ta*. Its negative apprehension of all things as empty or void (*sunya*) of reality is at bottom a positive way of realizing all things as ultimate reality or Nirvana itself. So it is that Mahayana Buddhism proclaims and practices compassion (*karuna*) as the primary reflection of the Void. For a true realization of the ultimate identity of all beings necessarily results in a practice of total compassion. And the highest disciples of the Buddha—the Bodhisattvas— give themselves to compassion as their calling; for the Bodhisattva is one who has reached the threshold of Nirvana but who takes the vow of renouncing his own salvation until all beings have been saved. He voluntarily returns to the world of suffering and illusion (*samsara*) as a means of mediating salvation to all. Out of perfect indifference (egolessness) and perfect compassion (which is also egolessness), the Bodhisattva does not experience enlightenment and then pass on to final extinction and release. Rather, he stops at the brink of Nirvana, and thus he transcends the opposition and distinction between *samsara* and Nirvana. The vow of the Bodhisattva, to remain at the brink until all enter Nirvana before him, amounts to a vow to remain as he is forever. This vow symbolizes the Buddhist truth, as Heinrich Zimmer has noted, that *samsara* and Nirvana do not exist as opposites, for both are equally emptiness (*sunyata*), the Void.

Paradoxical as it may appear to the Western mind, emptiness and compassion are inextricably associated in Buddhism. When everything is known to be empty of "reality," then radical self-giving can become not only a possibility but rather a necessity of genuine or true existence. It is precisely because the self is unreal that it can be given to the other; it is precisely because all things are ultimately identical that compassion is the most authentic response to the true nature of reality. At bottom the doctrine of the Void is the Buddhist means of identifying love as the center of reality, a center which here becomes all in all. Finally, Buddhism itself dissolves in response to the ultimate and universal reality of love. For if nothing separates the realm of suffering and illusion from the goal of release, then there is no way from ignorance and entanglement to enlightenment and freedom. Not only is there no way to enlightenment or Nirvana, but there is no Enlightened One, no Buddha. Buddhism ultimately demands the destruction of all words, the dissolution of all concepts. Here, naming or conceptualization of any kind is apprehended as the product of an individual and differentiated thinking and experience. Both thinking and experience are incapable of grasping or reflecting the un-differentiated reality of *tathata*. Neither can reach to that still point where the dance of Nirvana and *samsara* takes place—where Nirvana and *samsara* are one. All the higher expressions of Oriental vision culminate in a reali-zation of the One or the All, and total compassion is the Buddhist embodiment of that All. But Buddhist love can never truly be named or understood: it can only be im-mediately realized in a total point or moment which must appear to an alien vision as a void or nothingness.

How can the contemporary Christian respond to a Buddhist call and vision? He should know full well that to judge it to be empty and unreal is simply to record his own ignorance and illusion. Is there any way present to us of apprehending Buddhist compassion as a form or ground of Christian love? Have we not long since learned that the original eschatological ground and form of Chris-tian love is just as unreal and illusory to the modern mind as is the Buddhist vision of total compassion? Is it not possible that the equal unreality of both visions to us can be our way back to the lost and hidden ground of Chris-tian love? Certainly the greatest problem posed by Chris-tian love for us is that it seems to have no point of contact with what we know and experience as reality. Or does it? If we are to deal with the problem of our alienation from the call and reality of love, then we must take up the problem of Western dualism: the problem created by that uniquely Western chasm or fissure between the interior reality of selfhood and consciousness and the exterior reality of space and the world. It is this radical cleavage between the inner and the outer which wholly isolates an individual and interior consciousness from the call and reality of the other. Another can appear to us only as *the* other, an other which is wholly other from our selfhood, and alien to our consciousness and identity. It is precisely by knowing ourselves as isolated and apart that we experience another as an other, as one whose very distance from us guarantees and embodies what we know as our reality. Is there any way to that other so long as we remain imprisoned within our individual and interior identities? So long as we need the otherness of the other in order to be real ourselves?

The great call of innumerable forms of Western romanticism has been to make of our interior a totality or an All, an interior totality obliterating the distance of the outer and the without, and identifying the concrete individual as a face or mask of the inner and the within. One result of such romanticism is that the twentieth century has embodied the most powerful and the most comprehensive dualism in the history of the West. Not only have we evolved a public and institutional domain which is wholly estranged from the individual, but we have known a form of physical matter or energy which shows no signs of even a negative relationship to an interior or within, and have embodied a consciousness or a selfhood which appears to be neither within nor without. Indeed, the classical forms of Western dualism have collapsed in the twentieth century, and collapsed because the chasm which we once knew between an inner and an outer realm has now become so great that all meaning of inner as inner and outer as outer has disappeared. What meaning can love have for us when neither the intrinsic identity of the other nor the interior and individual identity of ourselves can appear and be real? It could even be said, as it has been said and envisioned by our seers, that selfhood as such has become wholly other for us. That selfhood which we can know and experience, whether our own or another's, is an alien selfhood, a selfhood empty of all that life or energy which we have been able to envision or name.

Can Buddhism give us a new way into the meaning of our dark and empty selfhood? Is it accidental that many of our modern seers—e.g., Joyce, Proust, and Beckett— have envisioned a totally exterior, empty, or alien self-hood, and thence envisioned its dissolution, thereby paralleling the Buddhist vision? If a Rilke and a Joyce, among others, have initiated us into a new interior or selfhood which is neither individual nor within, can we accept such an epiphany of ourselves as a way to a new and Christian love? Obviously these questions go far beyond the purview of this analysis, but they should lead us to see that Buddhism can point the way to a new meaning of Christian love, and it can do so at just those points wherein it is most alien to all we have understood as love. So long as we understand love as mutual and integral relationship between two isolated centers of consciousness and experience, then we shall remain closed to the advent of a new consciousness and experience which negates and transcends all such isolated and individual centers. So long as we attempt to practice compassion as an individual response to the unique and individual feeling of another—whether that other be an isolated individual or a distinct and individual group—we shall be closed to the advent of a new form of the other, a form in which individual identity, as we have known it, will have been negated and transcended. Buddhism can lead us away from our dualistic understanding of love, an understanding sealing the fissure between the within and the without and the chasm isolating the individual from the other. All our actual language about love, that is to say all that language which we can actually embody and speak, has invariably served to sanction these chasms and fissures. Thus the word "love" has become an obscene word in our time, a word that can be spoken only by the very innocent or the very corrupt. But speak it we must, even if we are therein forced to speak the language of a dark and empty innocence: for to abandon the language of love is to renounce the hope for compassion which we have been given in Christ.

As opposed to every romantic and dualistic understanding of love, a Christian apocalyptic vision envisions love as lying at the center of reality. True, the reality of which it is the heart and center is a new reality, a new creation or new aeon, and this reality dawns and becomes real only by way of the negation and reversal of an old reality. Apart from the negation of an old world or reality, a new reality cannot appear or be real; thus an eschatological form of love is inseparable from an act of radical negation. Does not the Buddhist vision of the Void as the way into the true and total reality of compassion provide us with a full parallel to eschatological negation as a way into the totality of love? But unlike all forms of Oriental vision, an eschatological vision evolves and becomes real only by way of an actual or real negation. Thus the old world or reality which is negated and reversed by eschatological negation is here apprehended as being neither illusory nor unreal. It is the actual or fallen reality of an old aeon or old creation which makes possible and actual a real act of negation and reversal. Accordingly, a Fall and a consequent fallenness are essential to eschatological and apocalyptic vision. Not only is fallenness essential to apocalyptic vision, but if that vision is to engage in a comprehensive and universal act and movement of negation, it must confront a total fallenness, a world or totality which is wholly alienated from an unfallen ground.

Is it not possible for the Christian to think of Buddhist compassion or *karuna* as the recovery and embodiment of such an unfallen ground? Buddhist compassion is not "other" than Christian love, it is rather its original ground or source. If Buddhism is a way back to a full recovery and total embodiment of a primordial All, then Christian-

ity is a way forward to a final and eschatological realization of that All. Yet, as we previously observed, it is only
the fall of an original Totality or All which can make possible either an eschatological movement of negation or a
final and apocalyptic "end." It is the disintegration, darkening, and dissolution of what the Buddhist knows as
total compassion which realizes and actualizes the Fall.
From the perspective of the Fall, that compassion is
wholly and finally lost, and there is no way to its recovery. But just as the Buddhist is given a way to an original
compassion by way of negating and dissolving all individual and actual consciousness and experience, so the
Christian is given a way to a final love or compassion by
way of actually negating and reversing everything which
is given to him by his history and experience. If the
Buddhist embodies total compassion by realizing the ultimate identity of all reality, then the Christian is called to
a new and total reality of love which can be realized only
by passing through an actual negation and reversal of a
fallen world. Just as Buddhist love is unreal if it appears
by way of the actuality and reality of the world, so Christian love is unreal if it appears apart from the brute reality and the full historical actuality of a fallen world.

Not only do the reality and actuality of a fallen world
make possible the actual act of eschatological negation,
but we should recognize that a total and radical negation
is a realization of an eschatological and Christian love.
Love, as the Christian has been given it in Christ, is not
an acceptance and affirmation of the other. It is rather an

attack upon all the distance that creates the alien and the other, an assault upon the actual estrangement of a fallen condition. Christian love is illusory and demonic when it ignores or sets aside its fallen ground, attempting to bridge the unbridgeable by pity or feeling. In the context of the actuality of fallenness, pity is not only an illusory form of compassion, but is a barrier to the actualization of compassion. Pity can be a genuine expression of Buddhist compassion because a total expression of pity can effect a full identification with another. But pity can only be demonic when it is given expression in an actually fallen form of consciousness and experience: here there can be no realization of an actual identity with another, but only an assuagement of the bitterness and guilt of alienation. In a Christian context, pity can only lower the threshold of consciousness, obliterating all awareness of the actuality of otherness. So it is that Christian prophets, and, most particularly, modern prophets such as Dostoyevsky and Nietzsche, have violently attacked pity and feeling, as escapes from the actuality of the human condition.

What we know as pity and sympathy are perverse expressions of what the Buddhist knows as compassion. They give us the illusion of identity with another even while deepening our mutual estrangement. Only an actual obliteration of that estrangement can be given the name of compassion, an obliteration which actually negates the reality of estrangement. If Buddhist compassion negates such estrangement by reversing and dissolving all consciousness and experience—or by annihilating everything which we can know as consciousness and experience—can we come to understand that Christian compassion effects an actual transformation of consciousness and experience? Then compassion would be unreal and illusory so long as it fails to decisively effect a given form of identity and selfhood. Apart from an actual transformation of both consciousness and self-consciousness, Christian love is not only unrealized, but it is also illusory and unreal. Yet an actual transformation of consciousness cannot be identified with a reversal and dissolution of consciousness. The one is a negation and a forward-moving transcendence of a given form of consciousness and identity, whereas the other is a negation and a backward-moving reversal of the movement and activity of consciousness. Christian compassion is an actual and real transformation of consciousness and selfhood, whereas Buddhist compassion is a dissolution and annihilation of selfhood and self-consciousness. Therefore Christian compassion totally reverses the pity and compassion of the Buddha, even if this reversal is a dialectical reversal, a reversal embodying the "emptiness" of Buddhist compassion in the actuality of time and flesh.

IV ❋

If we can realize that Christian love is the total reversal of Buddhist compassion, then we can know the Buddha as the original name and identity of the New Jerusalem or the apocalyptic Christ. Nothing so alienates the Chris-

tian from his ground and source in Christ as a false or illusory image of Christ. The very fallenness of the human
condition, as the Christian knows it, inevitably confronts
the Christian with the temptation of denying and refusing every present or contemporary image and identity of
Christ. The name of Christ is then identified either with
the realm of a lost and dreamy innocence or with an historical or mythical figure from an infinitely distant time.
Yet, if we can know the Buddha as the original name of
Christ, then we can be freed from the temptation of identifying Christ only with a past or ancient time. To know
the Buddha as the primordial identity of Christ is to recognize that Christ cannot be truly present or real in any
time or world which presents itself only in the form of the
past. The sacred name of the Buddha is itself a total
name or image of the primordial Totality, and it draws
into itself every past reality or identity which it touches,
thereby absorbing every past name or identity into itself.
Accordingly, to accept the Buddha as the primordial or
original name of Christ is to accept the dissolution of
every other particular name or image of Christ. So likewise it is to accept the loss of all past and individual
forms of Christ; for the Buddha, as a total image of the
primordial All, is an unveiling of the true identity of
every past form of the sacred. Thus to know the Buddha
as the primordial Christ is to be free from the sacred
power or claim of a Christian past in any particular form,
and thus to be freed from a disintegrating and increasingly invisible form and image of Christ.

Insofar as we identify a Christian love with a love having its origin and identity in our past, we will accordingly be alienated from the actuality of Christian love for us. Inevitably, the word "love" immediately arouses negative associations within us. For we associate it both with a lost and irretrievable world of the past and with an unreal and illusory world of the present. Our actual words for love immediately reflect our banishment from its paradise, and to speak positively or affirmatively of love we must invite illusion or self-laceration. We may look upon this situation, however, as a sign that we have once again become open to a prophetic meaning of love, to a meaning and reality of love that is inseparable from an eschatological and total judgment. In the perspective of an eschatological judgment, we could look upon the presence of a negative or self-dissolving reality as an occasion for hope, as a call to an actual reversal and transformation of an existing form of consciousness and selfhood. What we have come to know as the emptiness and illusion of love could then be for us a way to the transcendence of selfhood, to the abolition of our isolated and fragmentary selfhood. Once the call and reality of love is uprooted and dissociated from every isolated center of consciousness, then the possibility vanishes of a movement from one isolated center of interiority to another. With the disappearance of an individual and interior form of love, we must look either with bitterness or with a hopeless nostalgia upon the love which was once present in our history. But the disintegration of love as we have known it is an essential presupposition for the appearance of a new and comprehensive form of love.

One of the most striking characteristics of modern visions of love is the negative form of their purity or passion. Not only have we been dislodged from our former apprehensions of love, but love itself has appeared as an alienating and dehumanizing negativity, a negativity which freezes or consumes the passion and identity of man. While earlier scholars and critics recorded the demise of the romantic tradition of love, now we can see that romantic love did not simply disappear or fade away; it rather reversed itself. Not even in Euripides or Dante or Shakespeare can we find such negative images of love as we have been given throughout virtually the whole body of modern literature. Even a Blake or a Dostoyevsky seems like an innocent in love when viewed from the perspective of the twentieth century, for the contemporary vision has lost even the memory of a garden of innocence. From Ibsen, Strindberg, and Chekhov to the later Lawrence, Beckett, and Sartre would seem to be a straight and inevitable line in the disintegration of both the meaning and the reality of love.

But lying between these horizons of our maelstrom are the new sacred visions of Mallarmé and the later Rilke, the comprehensive if inverted visions of selfhood in Proust and Joyce, and the ecstatic intimations of total transformation in visionaries as diverse as Eliot and Brecht. If ours is a time of apocalyptic vision, it is so above all in its vision of love, for the modern vision has rediscovered a total and apocalyptic form of love. Jerusalem is the biblical name of an apocalyptic totality of love, and Jerusalem has once again appeared in modern vision, albeit under a wide variety of masks and cloaks. We should remember, moreover, that Jerusalem is apprehended by way of images of both light and darkness, and the full light of Jerusalem can never appear apart from the prior advent of the deepest darkness. Apocalyptic light is illusory and unreal apart from its ground in a fallen darkness, and the redeeming body of Jerusalem is unreal apart from the emptiness and horror of its dark opposite. Consequently, an apocalyptic faith can rejoice in what we have been given as the pure negativity of love.

At no other point does Buddhism, and the Buddhist vision of compassion, seem to be so relevant to our situation. For if the full reality of the love which we have known now appears to us in the form of a negative totality, then Buddhism can be a way to the dissolution or erasure of that totality, to the absolute stilling of all active expressions of love or desire. If it is the activity and the temporality of a Western and Faustian will which have led to the horror and chaos of the twentieth century, then Buddhism offers a way to a stilling of that will, to an absolute silence and calm in which neither will nor desire will be present. Buddhist discipline centers upon images of pain and suffering as a way to the dissolution of the activity and the individual identity of selfhood, for to know the self as pain and suffering is to be prepared for liberation from the illusion of selfhood. May we not regard modern Western vision as such a discipline, as a preparation for the dissolution of selfhood by way of a total immersion in the darkness and horror of life? And not only the darkness of life, but above all the darkness of love, the horror of our profoundest dream and hope. Is the dark emptiness of what has appeared to us as love a sign for us of the emptiness of everything, of the illusion of everything which we have known as consciousness and experience, and of the ultimate nothingness of all which has been present to us as reality and world? Or is the brutal actuality of our darkness such that we can consign it to illusion only by also refusing the reality of everything which we have known as a source or ground of suffering and pain? Is the dark negativity of our emptiness so overwhelming that no way is present to us of celebrating emptiness as a mask of total bliss?

If we truly acknowledge the actuality of our darkness, then we shall refuse every call of a primordial bliss. How could we forget the fallenness of our condition, or know our actuality as a mask of a totality of love? Yet if Buddhism provides us with a genuine image and even memory of total compassion, then we can come to realize the possibility of a total compassion for us. Such a love can never assume the form of a primordial emptiness, for we are banished by our actual fallenness from the unity of the primordial Beginning, and can remember its paradise only as an alien and empty nothingness. If we are to know a compassion which is real to us, then it will be a love which is manifest upon the plane of actuality.

Thereby it will be real to a fallen and differentiated consciousness, and actual in the contingency and temporality of a fallen space and time. Consequently, the total love which we have been given and can seek is inseparable from a radical and total transformation of our given consciousness and selfhood. We must not imagine that it is possible to dissolve *our* selfhood in a primordial emptiness, or for us to seek a total compassion which is identical with a dissolution of consciousness and experience. On the contrary, a compassion which can be real to us is a love effecting an actual and real transformation of *our* identities and *our* experience. There is no possibility for us of remembering or recovering our original identity, unless that identity appears and is real in the form of our darkness. Buddhism may well give us an image of total compassion, but if that image is not to be yet another mirage in our experience, then it must appear in the form and arena of *our* fallenness.

Once we are open to the New Jerusalem as a total reversal of an original All, then we can be open to the actuality of our dark emptiness as a sign of the presence of the light of the apocalyptic Christ. The apocalyptic Christ or the New Jerusalem can never be real to us so long as we are closed to the full reality of our emptiness. But by knowing and experiencing our emptiness as actual and real, we can become open to an apocalyptic call to a final negation and transcendence of *our* consciousness and experience. That call will be empty and unreal to us insofar as we are bound to previous forms of consciousness, to forms of consciousness which can apprehend the integral reality or the inherent goodness of an actual and individual center of consciousness. Only a passage through a total or apocalyptic collapse or end of that center of consciousness can prepare the way for the comprehensive presence of the New Jerusalem. Indeed, an apocalyptic end of an actual center of consciousness can be identified theologically as an historical embodiment of the New Jerusalem. The compassion of an apocalyptic Christ is inseparable from the advent of an actual disintegration of consciousness and experience. Accordingly, visions of a new apocalyptic compassion must inevitably appear in the form of madness or chaos to all those who can still find life or hope in an individual center of consciousness.

Just as the eschatological call of Jesus embodied a radical assault upon every form of faith or hope which it encountered, so a contemporary apocalyptic vision will totally challenge all existing or previous forms of meaning and identity. Inevitably, a new apocalyptic vision has challenged the reality of our love, and challenged it in such a manner as to unveil the dark and empty negativity of everything which we can positively know or envision as love. Nor has a Dostoyevsky, a Nietzsche, a Strindberg, a Freud, or a Proust initiated us into an understanding of the simple illusion or emptiness of love. They have rather led us into a realization of the self-centered and self-lacerating perversion of everything which we have consciously and interiorly celebrated as the reality of love. Once we become open to the full negativity of our isolated and in-

dividual form of selfhood, then everything which any individual form of consciousness has celebrated and
affirmed will appear to us to be empty of all positive hope
and meaning. In form, Nietzsche's vision of Eternal Recurrence is identical with the Buddhist vision of the Void.
But whereas the Buddhist vision of the Void is an embodiment of total compassion, that new and total form of
chaos and emptiness which Nietzsche envisioned as Eternal Recurrence, would seem to have no point of contact
with anything which truly can be named as love. Or can
it? Does it not take us into the very center of a fallen consciousness and experience? And are not the negation and
transcendence of that center the primary arena for the
expression of an apocalyptic love? If the embodiment of
an apocalyptic compassion is inseparable from the end of
an actual center of consciousness, then can we not say
that a genuine vision of such an end is by necessity a vision of a new and total love?

The contemporary mind is all too naturally inclined to
identify apocalyptic vision with visions of total darkness
and horror. Now there can be no doubt that we have
been given visions of such darkness and horror; furthermore, these visions of darkness have been fullest when
the modern mind and imagination have been most fully
"awake." Nevertheless, the fact remains that genuine
apocalyptic vision embodies visions of both total darkness
and total light. Here, darkness is finally only the immediate or initial expression of light. Or, rather, darkness is
most dark when it is envisioned as having come to an

end, and that end is identical with the total triumph of light. But an apocalyptic "light" can never truly appear apart from a comprehensive vision of the end of darkness. Should we not then expect that visions of light will appear to be only visions of darkness? And will this not most particularly be so when a contemporary vision of light is manifest to an individual and interior center of consciousness? Yet apart from the radical negation or actual dissolution of all individual and interior identity and meaning, there can be no end of an actual center of consciousness, and thus no vision of the New Jerusalem.

If the New Jerusalem is the historical actualization of a total but dialectical reversal of an original All, then that All will itself be present in a new and reverse form or identity. The Hell which has appeared and is appearing in our world as a Totality or an All must finally be recognized as a reverse or inverted form of a primordial Heaven. Not until Hell appears and is real as a Totality or All will an original Heaven finally be emptied: for the actualization of the totality of Hell is inseparable from the dissolution or emptying of Heaven. The totality of Hell necessarily embodies the totality of Heaven, and total visions of Hell must finally become manifest as visions of a totally new and reverse or inverted form of what was once manifest and real as Heaven. If the Christian has now lost all sense of the original meaning and identity of Heaven, then this may be seen as an inevitable consequence of the appearance of a totally reversed form of Heaven, of the appearance of Heaven in the form of Hell.

The apocalpytic Christ who is appearing to us is present at the center of Hell, and we can be open to his presence only by opening ourselves to the finality and totality of Hell. Yet only by passing through an actual negation of every form of consciousness and experience which is open to an original or primordial form of Heaven can we ourselves become open to the historical actualization of Hell. Only the final and total loss of Heaven can open us to the advent of the Christ who has fully and finally descended into Hell. Only the final self-annihilation of an actual and individual center of consciousness can make possible the advent of an actual and universal consciousness, a consciousness embodying the original as the final All, the primordial Totality as the New Jerusalem.

If the final triumph of Hell is identical with the final emptying of an original Heaven, then an actual way to Heaven can only be real to us as a way to Hell. Just as we have lost all living or vital images of a heavenly or primordial Christ, so we have been given new and comprehensive images of a Christ who is totally here and now, who is present at the center of darkness or Hell. So long as we remain open to the call and memory of Heaven, we will remain closed to the presence and identity of the Christ who has fully descended into Hell. But if Christ has finally descended into Hell, then an actual and present way to Christ will be a way into the center of Hell. Only by knowing Hell as the arena and realm of Christ can we freely accept Hell as our destiny, and thereby accept the annihilation of everything we have known as consciousness and experience as a total epiphany of Christ. Once Christ is known as the source and ground of a total transformation of consciousness and experience, then the loss of all we have known as identity and selfhood can be accepted and affirmed as the realization of the presence and compassion of Christ. True darkness can then be known as the fruit of compassion, and the actual death of an individual center of consciousness can then be celebrated as the self-annihilating presence of the universal Christ. Now the way "up" will be the way "down": an ascension to Heaven will be *identical* with a descent into Hell.

Index

✳